THE Right TO Dignity

Fidel Castro AND THE Nonaligned Movement

Edited by
David Deutschmann
and
Deborah Shnookal

Photographs by
Osvaldo Salas

Ocean Press
Australia
1989

The publisher gratefully acknowledges the assistance of the José Martí Foreign Languages Publishing House of Havana, Cuba, in the preparation of this book.

Cover photo: Osvaldo Salas

ISBN 1 875284 03 6 cloth;

ISBN 1 875284 02 8 paper

First edition, 1989

Published by Ocean Press
GPO Box 3279 GG, Melbourne, Victoria 3001, Australia

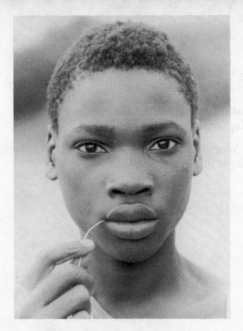

Contents

Preface

'We represent the great majority of humanity. We are united by the determination to defend the cooperation between our countries, free national and social development, sovereignty, security, equality and self-determination.

'It is imperative to do away with the enormous inequality that separates the developed countries from the developing countries. We are struggling to eradicate poverty, hunger, disease and illiteracy from which hundreds of millions of human beings still suffer.

'We aspire to a new world order, one based on justice, on equity and on peace. One that will replace the unjust and unequal system that prevails today.'

(Fidel Castro to the United Nations 34th General Assembly, October, 1979, on behalf of the Movement of Nonaligned Countries)

v

The Movement of Nonaligned Countries was founded in September, 1961 in Belgrade, Yugoslavia, by more than 300 delegates representing 25 countries of Asia, Africa and Latin America.

Composed overwhelmingly of those countries emerging as newly independent after World War II, the Nonaligned Movement in its first declaration noted a transition was taking place 'from an old order based on domination to a new order based on cooperation between nations.' The Movement saw its role in this situation as 'one of the most important factors for safeguarding world peace.'

By the time of the Second Summit in Cairo, 1964, the Nonaligned Movement had nearly doubled in size. Of the 22 new member nations, 20 were newly independent African states. By the Fourth Summit in Algiers in 1973 the Movement had 75 members, making up nearly two-thirds of the United Nations' membership and over 90 percent of countries which had won independence since 1945.

Reviewing the first 20 years of the Nonaligned Movement in 1981, Fidel Castro wrote: 'It was to the credit of the founders of our Movement and proof of their great political foresight to have linked the struggle for the universal, just peace the peoples were striving for to the struggle to eliminate the old order based on domination and oppression that stubbornly persisted and was threatening peace.' It is still the case today, Castro continued, 'that true peace can only be attained in a world where domination by colonialism, imperialism and neocolonialism in all their manifestations are radically eliminated.'

Therefore, Castro concluded, 'the Movement represents the clear majority of the international community and expresses the militant political positions of the underdeveloped and developing countries.'

The struggle for peace and the need for development have been recurring themes taken up by the Nonaligned Movement throughout its history. As Fidel Castro summarized the question at the Harare Summit in 1986, 'There can be no development without peace nor can there be peace without development for the immense majority of the world's peoples.'

As a founding member of the Movement of Nonaligned Countries, Cuba was at one time its only Latin American member. This was less than three years after the rebel forces led by Fidel Castro had overthrown the U.S.-backed Batista dictatorship on

January 1, 1959. Cuba has since emerged as one of the most influential members of the Movement, reflected in the holding of the Sixth Summit in Havana in 1979. Its prestige and influence within the movement has been greatly increased due to its unstinting solidarity with the Third World. For example, Cuba, a country of ten million people, itself struggling to overcome the effects of centuries of colonial rule and exploitation and the victim of a total economic blockade by the United States, by 1979 had twice as many doctors working overseas as the UN World Health Organization.

Cuba's readiness to help Angola defend itself from South African aggression—shown by the more than 300,000 Cuban internationalists who volunteered during the 13-year mission— as well as its commitment to the cause of Namibian independence, have played a part in changing the history of Africa. It has won Cuba the respect of all opponents of racism and colonialism throughout the world.

This book is a collection of the interventions by Fidel Castro to the major gatherings of the Movement of Nonaligned Countries from 1973 to 1986, made both as president of Cuba and as Movement chair (1979-83). They reflect the consistent themes and concerns of the Nonaligned Movement in the past two decades. They review, as well as anticipate, the major international events of this period.

Fidel Castro is today one of the most outspoken defenders of the rights of the Third World, as his speeches included in this volume clearly testify. In addressing the United Nations on behalf of the Nonaligned Movement in 1979, Fidel Castro said:

'Human rights are very often spoken of, but we must also speak of humanity's rights.

'Why should some people go barefoot, so that others may ride in expensive cars?

'Why should some live only 35 years, so that others may live 70?

'Why should some be miserably poor, so that others may be exaggeratedly rich?

'I speak on behalf of the children of the world who don't even have a piece of bread. I speak on behalf of the sick who lack medicine. I speak on behalf of those who have been denied the right to life and to human dignity.

'Some countries possess abundant resources, others have nothing. What is their fate? To starve? To be eternally poor?

Why then civilization? Why then the conscience of man? Why then the United Nations? Why then the world?'

It is necessary to acknowledge the valuable assistance received in the preparation of this book from the José Martí Foreign Languages Publishing House of Havana and its director, Félix Sautié. José Amieva of the José Martí Publishing House was particularly helpful in researching background to the Movement of Nonaligned Countries.

The support we received from Javier Salado was crucial for the speedy preparation of this book.

The photographs featured in this book are by the outstanding Cuban photographer, Osvaldo Salas. His photographic portraits have been widely acclaimed internationally and it is from this collection that we have chosen a range of Salas photographs from his travels through Africa, Asia and Latin America. These photographs graphically depict the themes taken up by the Nonaligned Movement contained in this book.

David Deutschmann
Deborah Shnookal
August, 1989

Abbreviations

ANC	African National Congress
CENTO	Central Treaty Organization
CIA	Central Intelligence Agency (United States)
FAO	Food and Agricultural Organization
FMLN	Farabundo Marti National Liberation Front (El Salvador)
FSLN	Sandinista National Liberation Front (Nicaragua)
GATT	General Agreement on Tariffs and Trade
ILO	International Labor Organization
IMF	International Monetary Fund
MPLA	People's Movement for the Liberation of Angola
NATO	North Atlantic Treaty Organization
NLF	National Liberation Front (Vietnam)
OAU	Organization of African Unity
OECD	Organization for Economic Cooperation and Development
OPEC	Organization of Petroleum Exporting Countries
PLO	Palestine Liberation Organization
SALT	Strategic Arms Limitation Talks

SWAPO	South West Africa People's Organization
UNCTAD	United Nations Conference on Trade and Development
UNESCO	United Nations Educational, Scientific and Cultural Organization
UNICEF	United Nations International Children's Emergency Fund
UNIDO	United Nations Industrial Development Organization
UNITA	National Union for the Total Independence of Angola
WHO	World Health Organization

Chronology

1953

July 26: Fidel Castro leads a group of young rebels in an attack on the Moncada military barracks in Santiago de Cuba, marking the start of the insurrection against the Batista dictatorship in Cuba.

1954

April: Colonel Gamal Abdel Nasser becomes prime minister in Egypt. He later becomes president.

June 18: Government of Jacobo Arbenz is overthrown in Guatemala by CIA-backed coup.

1955

April 18-24: The Asian African Conference is held in Bandung, Indonesia. Twenty-nine countries from Asia and Africa participate. Prominent at this meeting are President Sukarno of Indonesia, Prime Minister Jawaharlal Nehru of India and Nasser.

1956

July: Nasser meets with Nehru and Yugoslav leader Josip Broz Tito in Belgrade.

October-December: Following the nationalization of the Suez Canal on July 26, Britain, France and Israel attack Egypt.

1959

January 1: Batista dictatorship is overthrown in Cuba by the rebel forces led by Fidel Castro.

1960

July 1: Popular referendum in Ghana proclaims a republic following independence in 1957; Kwame Nkrumah is elected president.

September: Nasser, Nehru, Tito, Nkrumah and Sukarno meet at the 15th General Assembly of the United Nations.

1961

February: Patrice Lumumba, president of the newly-independent Republic of the Congo (now Zaire), is assassinated.

April 17-19: A CIA-sponsored invasion of Cuba by 1,200 mercenaries landing at Playa Giron (Bay of Pigs) is defeated within 72 hours.

June 5-12: Preparatory meeting for the First Conference of the Nonaligned Countries is held in Cairo, Egypt. Yugoslavia is chosen as the host for the summit.

September 1-6: First Summit Conference of Nonaligned Countries in Belgrade elects Tito as chair of the Movement. More than 300 delegates representing 25 member nations from Asia, Africa and Latin America participate. Cuba is the only Latin American country represented.

1962

March: Algerian liberation forces sign cease-fire with France after eight-year war. France agrees to recognize Algerian independence.

October 22-28: U.S. President Kennedy initiates 'Cuban missile crisis' denouncing Cuba's acquisition of nuclear-capable missiles. Washington imposes a naval blockade on Cuba and threatens the Soviet Union with nuclear war. Cuba responds by mobilizing the people. Soviet Premier Khrushchev agrees to remove the missiles in exchange for a U.S. pledge not to invade Cuba.

1964

January 9: Panamanian students raise their national flag in the Canal Zone. U.S. troops open fire on the crowd killing 25 and wounding at least 500 protesters.

March 23-June 15: UN Conference on Trade and Development (UNCTAD) meets in Geneva, where the Group of 77 is formed as a caucus of developing countries.

April 1: The CIA overthrows President Goulart of Brazil and installs a military regime.

May 27: Nehru dies.

October 5-10: Second Summit of the Nonaligned Countries in Cairo elects Nasser as chair of the Movement. Forty-seven member nations attend as well as 10 observer countries. Of the 22 new members, 20 are African states.

1965

April: U.S. sends marines to Dominican Republic.

April-December: Che Guevara carries out mission in the Congo to support the independence fighters there.

August: First Cuban internationalist volunteers arrive in Africa to support the government of Congo-Brazzaville and the People's Movement for the Liberation of Angola (MPLA).

October: Government of President Sukarno is overthrown in Indonesia by U.S.-backed military coup.

1966

U.S. war against Vietnam intensifies.

January: Tricontinental Conference of Solidarity with the Peoples of Asia, Africa and Latin America held in Havana.

February 24: CIA instigates the ouster of President Nkrumah of Ghana.

1967

June: Six-day Arab-Israeli war.

October 8: Che Guevara is assassinated in La Higuera, Bolivia.

1968

January-February: Tet offensive launched against the U.S.-backed Saigon regime by the Vietnamese National Liberation Front (NLF).

1970

September 4: Popular Unity government led by Salvador Allende elected in Chile.

September 8: Nasser dies.

September 8-10: Third Summit Conference of Nonaligned Countries takes place in Lusaka, Zambia. The 53 member nations participating elect President Kenneth Kaunda of Zambia as Movement chair.

1972

August 8-11: Ministerial conference of Nonaligned Movement is held in Georgetown, Guyana with 59 members attending and nine national liberation movements present as observers. This is the first major Movement meeting in Latin America.

1973

August 20-25: On the eve of the Algerian Summit a meeting on the worsening economic situation in developing countries takes place in Santiago de Chile to express solidarity with the Allende government.

September 5-9: Fourth Summit Conference of Nonaligned Movement in Algiers elects Houari Boumedienne of Algeria as chair. This summit is attended by 75 member nations, including 22 new members. The Nonaligned Countries now make up nearly two-thirds of UN membership and over 90 percent of countries which had won independence since World War II. Eight countries, all from the Caribbean and Latin America, participate as observers at the Algiers Summit. A 15-member coordinating bureau is elected consisting of Algeria, Cuba, Guyana, Kuwait, Liberia, Malaysia, Nepal, Peru, Tanzania, Senegal, Somalia, Sri Lanka, Syria, Yugoslavia and Zaire, plus India and Mali.

September 11: President Allende is overthrown in Chile by CIA-backed coup led by General Pinochet.

October: Arab-Israeli war.

1974

April 25: Downfall of fascist dictatorship in Portugal.

September 12: New Portuguese government officially recognizes the independence of its former colony, Guinea-Bissau.

1975

March 17-19: Meeting of the coordinating bureau is held in Havana where Fidel Castro gives closing speech.

April 30: Final victory of national liberation forces in Vietnam, followed by defeat of U.S.-backed regimes in Cambodia and Laos.

June 25: Popular Republic of Mozambique proclaims independence from Portugal.

July: Sao Tome and Principe gain independence. Cape Verde declares independence.

November: Cuba responds to an MPLA request for military aid following the South African invasion of Angola (October 23). People's Republic of Angola declares independence (November 11) with Agostinho Neto as its first president. Combined Angolan and Cuban forces defeat South Africa by March 1976.

1976

July 2: Proclamation of the Socialist Republic of Vietnam.

August 16-19: Fifth Summit of Nonaligned Movement. Prime Minister Sirimavo Bandaranaike of Sri Lanka is elected chair by the 86 members present at the Colombo Summit. The coordinating bureau is increased from 15 to 25 members divided by regions as follows: Africa, 12; Asia, 8; Latin America, 4; Europe, 1.

1978

December 27: Boumedienne dies.

1979

January 7: Vietnamese support the popular overthrow of Pol Pot regime in Kampuchea.

February: Iranian revolution ousts Shah.

March 13: New Jewel Movement led by Maurice Bishop defeats Gairy dictatorship in Grenada.

July 19: Nicaraguan masses led by Sandinista Front overthrow Somoza regime.

August: On the eve of the Havana Summit, Washington attempts to undermine Cuba's authority within the Movement with charges about Soviet troops in Cuba.

September 3-9: Sixth Summit of Nonaligned Countries takes place in Havana. All but two of the 95 members attend and elect Fidel Castro as Movement chair. Castro gives the opening and closing addresses to the conference.

October 12: Fidel Castro speaks to the 34th session of the United Nations' General Assembly on behalf of the Nonaligned Countries.

1980

April: Zimbabwe gains independence with Robert Mugabe elected prime minister.

May 4: Death of Tito.

1981

February 11: Cuban foreign minister Isidoro Malmierca reads a message from Fidel Castro to the 20th anniversary meeting of the Nonaligned Movement in New Delhi.

1982

April: Britain provokes war with Argentina over the Malvinas Islands.

June: Israel invades Lebanon.

September: Massacre of Palestinians at refugee camps of Sabra and Shatilla, in Beirut, Lebanon.

1983

March 7-13: Seventh Summit of Nonaligned Movement in New Delhi elects Indian Prime Minister Indira Gandhi as chair. As out-going chair Fidel Castro makes the opening address to the 99 members participating.

October 19: Bishop government of Grenada is overthrown.

October 25: U.S. troops invade Grenada.

1984

October 31: Indira Gandhi assassinated.

1985

August: Five day conference in Havana on the Third World debt calls for restructuring the relations between debtor and creditor nations. The conference is attended by 1,200 delegates representing 37 countries.

1986

September 1-6: Eighth Summit in Harare, Zimbabwe elects Robert Mugabe as chair of the Movement of Nonaligned Countries. More than 100 member nations and national liberation movements participate. Fidel Castro presents two speeches: the first on behalf of the Latin American group and the second on behalf of Cuba.

'Vietnam taught all oppressed nations that no force can defeat a people that is determined to fight for its freedom. The struggle in Vietnam reinforced the respect and dignity of all our peoples.'

The meaning of nonalignment

Mr Chairman; Distinguished heads of state and government; Representatives of the heroic national liberation movements; Delegates:

In expressing to you, Comrade Boumedienne, to your compatriots and the distinguished representatives of the peoples meeting at this conference the greetings of the Cuban delegation, we would like to emphasize the meaning we assign to the fact that this Fourth Conference of Nonaligned Countries is taking place in Algeria, whose people, with their heroic and sustained struggle, awakened the admiration and served as encouragement for the countries that have fought for their national independence against the oppressors.

I want to remind you that Cuba is a socialist country, Marxist-Leninist, whose final objective is communism. We are proud of this! On the basis of that concept of human society, we determine our domestic and foreign policies. We are, above all, loyal to the principles of proletarian internationalism, and my words will be consistent with those ideas. All revolutionaries are duty-bound to defend their views in valiant fashion, and that is what I propose to do here as briefly as possible, since I don't intend to speak for an hour and a half, in order to respect the rights of others to speak at the conference, too.

There has been talk at this conference of the different ways of dividing the world. To our way of thinking, the world is divided into capitalist and socialist countries, imperialist and neocolonialized

This speech by Fidel Castro was given to the Fourth Summit Conference of the Movement of Nonaligned Countries in Algiers, Algeria. The conference was held 5–9 September 1973. It was the first summit or meeting of the Nonaligned Movement that was attended by Fidel Castro.

countries, colonialist and colonialized countries, reactionary and progressive countries—governments, in a word, that back imperialism, colonialism, neocolonialism and racism, and governments that oppose imperialism, colonialism, neocolonialism and racism.

This seems to us to be basic in the issue of alignment and nonalignment, because there is nothing exempting us in any way from our central obligation of steadfastly fighting the crimes committed against humanity.

The Movement has grown without any question, and that is a source of satisfaction to us, as is the case of Latin America, when the presence here of three new states—Peru, Chile and Argentina—is due to progressive political changes in those countries. But the quality and not the number is what should take primacy for the purposes of this Movement if we really mean to wield moral and political force before the peoples of the world. If this is not the case, we run the risk that the reactionary forces could succeed in penetrating its ranks to thwart its aims, and that the unity and prestige of the nonaligned countries could be irremediably lost.

Although the economic interests of the countries we represent take on justified and necessary importance, the political criteria we uphold will continue to be a basic factor in our activity.

In this political terrain there has been an observable tendency during the months of preparation leading up to this conference that unquestionably militates against our cause and serves only imperialist interests, to seek to pit the nonaligned countries against the socialist camp.

The theory of "two imperialisms", one headed by the United States and the other allegedly by the Soviet Union, encouraged by the theoreticians of capitalism, has been echoed at times deliberately and at others through ignorance of history and the realities of the present-day world, by leaders and spokesmen of nonaligned countries. This is fostered, of course, by those who regrettably betray the cause of internationalism from supposedly revolutionary positions.

In certain political and economic documents drafted for this conference we've seen that current come to the fore in one way or another, with different shadings. The revolutionary government of Cuba will always oppose that current in all circumstances. That is why we find ourselves obliged to deal with this delicate matter as an essential issue.

There are some who, with patent historic injustice and ingratitude, forgetting the real facts and disregarding the profound, unbridgeable abyss between the imperialist regime and socialism. They try to ignore the glorious, heroic and extraordinary services rendered to the human race by the Soviet people, as if the collapse of the colossal system of colonial rule implanted in the world up to World War II and the conditions that made possible the liberation of scores of peoples heretofore under direct colonial subjugation, the disappearance of capitalism in large parts of the world and the holding at bay of the aggression and insatiable voracity of imperialism—as if all that, had nothing to do with the glorious October Revolution!

How can the Soviet Union be labeled imperialist? Where are its monopoly corporations? Where is its participation in the multinational companies? What factories, what mines, what oilfields does it own in the underdeveloped world? What worker is exploited in any country of Asia, Africa, or Latin America by Soviet capital?

The economic cooperation that the Soviet Union provides to Cuba and many other countries comes not from the sweat and the sacrifice of the exploited workers of other peoples, but from the sweat and efforts of the Soviet workers.

Others regret the fact that the first socialist state in history has become a military and economic power. We underdeveloped and plundered countries must not regret this. Cuba rejoices that this is so. Without the October Revolution and without the immortal feat of the Soviet people, who first withstood imperialist intervention and blockade and later defeated the fascist aggression at the cost of 20 million dead, who have developed their technology and economy at an unbelievable price in efforts and heroism without exploiting the labor of a single worker of any country on the face of the earth—without them, the end of colonialism and the balance of power in the world that favored the heroic struggles of so many peoples for their liberation wouldn't have been possible. Not for a moment can we forget that the guns with which Cuba crushed the Playa Girón [Bay of Pigs] mercenaries and defended itself from the United States; the arms in the hands of the Arab peoples, with which they withstand imperialist aggression; those used by the African patriots against Portuguese colonialism; and those taken up by the Vietnamese in their heroic, extraordinary and victorious struggle came from the socialist countries, especially from the Soviet Union.

The very resolutions of the Nonaligned Countries aid us in understanding the dividing line in international politics today.

What state have those resolutions condemned from Belgrade to

Lusaka for its aggression in Vietnam and all Indochina? The imperialist United States. Whom do we accuse of arming, supporting and continuing to maintain the Israeli aggressor state in its rapacious war against the Arab countries and in its cruel occupation of the territories where the Palestinians have the right to live? We accuse U.S. imperialism. Against whom did the nonaligned countries protest over the invasion and blockade of Cuba and the intervention in the Dominican Republic and for maintaining bases at Guantánamo, in Panama and in Puerto Rico against the will of their peoples? Who was behind the murder of Lumumba? Who supports the killers of Amilcar Cabral? Who helps to maintain in Zimbabwe a white racist state and turn South Africa into a reserve of black men and women in conditions of semislavery? Who backs Portuguese colonialism against the peoples of Guinea-Bissau and Cape Verde, Angola and Mozambique? In all these cases, the culprit is the same: U.S. imperialism.

When our resolutions list the millions of dollars, pounds, francs or marks that leave the developing neocolonialized or colonialized countries as a consequence of plundering investments and onerous loans, they condemn imperialism and not any other social system. It is not possible to change reality with equivocal expression.

Any attempt to pit the nonaligned countries against the socialist camp is profoundly counterrevolutionary and benefits only imperialist interests. Inventing a false enemy can have only one aim, to evade the real enemy.

The success and the future of the Nonaligned Movement will depend on its refusal to allow itself to be penetrated, confused or deceived by imperialist ideology. Only the closest alliance among all the progressive forces of the world will provide us with the strength needed to overcome the still-powerful forces of imperialism, colonialism, neocolonialism and racism and to wage a successful fight for peace and justice of all the peoples of the world. With the preoccupying, increasing needs for sources of energy and raw materials on the part of the developed capitalist countries in order to maintain the absurd consumer societies they have created, were it not for the extraordinary containing power of the socialist camp, imperialism would carve up the world all over again. New wars would plague the human race, and many of the independent countries that today belong to this Movement would not even exist. Right now there are leading circles in the United States that are pushing for military intervention in the Middle East if fuel requirements warrant it.

Any estrangement from the socialist camp means weakening and exposing ourselves to the mercy of the still-powerful forces of imperialism. It would be a stupid strategy, a case of severe political shortsightedness.

Mr Chairman, Latin America notes with concern the way that Brazil, under U.S. sponsorship, is building up a military might that goes way beyond the needs of its rulers to employ armed brutality, murder, torture and imprisonment against its people. Brazil is visibly growing into a military enclave in the heart of Latin America at the service of U.S. imperialism. The government of Brazil— which, along with that of the United States, took part in the invasion of the Dominican Republic and then with the same partner worked to overthrow the progressive government of Bolivia and recently helped to implant a reactionary dictatorship in Uruguay— is not only a tool of the United States but is gradually becoming an imperialist state. Today it has an observer status at this confer- ence, as has Bolivia. We hope that such governments, under which some peoples of our hemisphere still suffer, are never admitted to the Nonaligned Movement.

There has been considerable talk here of the situation prevailing in Southeast Asia and in the Middle East; of the peoples oppressed and held by Portugese colonialism; of the brutal racist repression in South Africa, Zimbabwe and Namibia.

U.S. imperialism continues to back the neocolonial regime in South Vietnam, which refuses to comply with the Paris Agree- ments, and the puppet governments of Lon Nol in Cambodia; Israel mocks the United Nations resolutions and refuses to return the territories it occupied by force; Portugal, with the backing of the United States and NATO, scorns world opinion and the resolutions against it adopted by international bodies. The racist governments not only step up repression but threaten other African states.

These are bitter, outrageous truths that put the strength, unity and will to struggle of the nonaligned countries to the test. We who are meeting here are the leaders and representatives of more than 70 states. Let us enact concrete measures and agreements to isolate and defeat the aggressors. Let us support in a determined, steadfast manner, the Arab peoples under attack and the heroic people of Palestine; the fighters for the independence of Guinea- Bissau and Cape Verde, Angola and Mozambique; the oppressed peoples of South Africa, Zimbabwe and Namibia! Let us fight consistently against the imperialist countries that aid and abet these crimes! Let all of us nonaligned countries recognize the Provisional Revolutionary Government of South Vietnam and let us give our full support to it in the struggle for compliance with the Paris Agreements! Let us back the patriots of Laos and Cambodia, and no force in the world will be able to prevent the solution of these problems that affect our peoples in the Middle East, Africa and Southeast Asia!

The true strength and depth of the Movement of Nonaligned Countries will be measured by the firmness of our actions regarding these problems. Cuba will back with the greatest determination the agreements adopted to that effect, even if to do so calls for contribution of our blood.

We cannot ignore the Democratic Republic of Vietnam. That people, a thousand times heroic, has undergone the most devastating war of aggression. Millions of tons of bombs were dropped on their economic facilities, cities, towns, schools and hospitals. Their self-sacrificing and victorious struggle against imperialist aggression has served the interests of the entire human race. We must not settle for expressions of sympathy. Right now, that admirable country is confronting the difficult work of reconstruction. We propose to the nonaligned countries that we take part in the rebuilding of North Vietnam, with each of us making a contribution to the extent of our possibilities. This would provide a new and revolutionary dimension to the nonaligned nations in the field of international solidarity.

The nonaligned countries must express their solidarity with Zambia and Tanzania against South African and Rhodesian aggression. We must also support the Democratic People's Republic of Korea in its efforts to attain the peaceful reunification of Korean people. We must offer the Panamanian people full support in their just struggle for sovereignty in the Canal Zone. We must provide solidarity with the people of Chile in the face of imperialist plotting. We must join with Argentina in its just demand for the return of the usurped Malvinas Islands. And we must defend the right of the people of Puerto Rico to full sovereignty.

Our country must put up with the humiliating presence of a U.S. base [Guantánamo] on a part of our territory, maintained by force completely against the will of our people, who confront a rigorous and criminal economic blockade by the United States. Despite that, the Cuban people stand firm and are successfully building socialism right at the gateway to the United States. Our country has been able to resist because it has carried out a genuine revolution that radically wiped out all forms of exploitation of man by man, building upon that base a lofty fighting morale and a solid, indestructible unity.

When there is a real desire to free a country from imperialist exploitation, then the people must also be freed from the plunder of the fruits of their labor by the feudal lords, the landholders, the oligarchs and the social parasites of all kinds.

We also ask for your solidarity with the Cuban people.

If an understanding with the socialist countries is a vital factor for our victory, unity among the nations fighting for independence and development is its indispensable condition. We support all pronouncements in favor of greater unity of the nonaligned on the principal problems of international life that are included in the different motions presented to the conference. But we are concerned—more than concerned, we become indignant—when we see that a leader of the stature of Sékou Touré [of Guinea] must defend himself not only against the Portuguese colonialists but also against conspiracies promoted right inside his own underdeveloped Africa.

Our faith in certain unity declarations and postulates wanes when we see that the People's Republic of the Congo and the Republic of Somalia are not free from threats by other African forces and we note the difficulties of the Revolutionary Government of the Democratic People's Republic of Yemen in overcoming hostilities that may well stem from Washington but which are carried out from other areas closer at hand.

All of this shows that our true unity depends not on circumstantial nonalignment but on a deeper, more lasting identity, an identity stemming from revolutionary principles, a common anti-imperialist program and an aspiration to substantial, conclusive social transformations.

This is Cuba's position. The point of view that I have just outlined will surely not be shared by all the leaders meeting here, but I have complied with my duty to express them with respect and with loyalty toward all of you.

Thank you very much.

7

'Some would like to solve the tragic problem of humanity with drastic measures to reduce the population. They want to blame under-development on to the population explosion. But the population explosion is not the cause, but the result of underdevelopment.'

The economic crisis and the Third World

Distinguished members of the coordinating bureau of the Nonaligned Countries; Distinguished observers:

It is a signal honor for our people that this meeting of the coordinating bureau has taken place in Cuba.

We appreciate in all its worth the presence of the representatives of the valiant and fighting peoples that have distinguished themselves internationally for their contribution to the struggle for the independence and progress of their homelands, world peace and the success of the noble objectives of the Movement that brings us here.

The coordinating bureau meets a year and a half after the Algiers Summit Conference, and each day that has passed since then confirms the importance and the role of the Nonaligned Movement and the diagnosis of the international situation made in the resolutions.

Important international events have occurred since then, some adverse, many favorable. Immediately after that event was the criminal fascist coup that imperialism perpetrated in Chile. We recall that President Allende was unable to come to Algiers because at that time he was confronting the subversive actions and sabotage of the reaction. Foreign Minister Clodomiro Almeyda and other spokesmen of the progressive movement denounced the actions and pointed out the active intervention of the imperialist government of the United States in Chile's internal policy. President Allende's cause found deep sympathy and broad solidarity in that conference. How hard it was to imagine that barely 72 hours after the closing of the Algiers Summit, President Allende would

At a ministerial meeting of the Movement of Nonaligned Countries held in Havana, Cuba, Fidel Castro presented this speech.

die heroically, resisting the fascist blow that put an end to that admirable effort to make the revolution through institutional and peaceful means, an effort which the world followed with particular interest. Today, CIA participation in those events is no longer simply a charge or a hypothesis, because it has been admitted and, what is worse, justified by the United States government itself.

The nonaligned countries have joined the enormous wave of world solidarity with the Chilean people that followed the fascist coup, along with the socialist countries which almost unanimously broke with the usurper regime, and the world revolutionary and progressive movement. The fascist junta, today internationally isolated, crushingly discredited, repudiated by the masses and drowned in the blood of its own people, has no alternative other than defeat.

Following close on the heels of those events, the heroic battle of the Arab peoples to liberate the occupied territories took place in October 1973, ending the myth of the invincibility of the aggressor Israeli state, giving rise to a new correlation of forces in the Middle East and also to a new phase in the struggle of the Arab peoples to recover their legitimate territories and restore the national right of the heroic Palestinians, criminally oppressed and expelled from their native land.

Today imperialism is making efforts to counteract this situation maneuvering perfidiously to divide the Arab countries, isolate the courageous Syrian people, cheat the Palestinians of their rights and extend its presence and influence in the Middle East, in order to impose the onerous peace conditions that most suit its interests and those of its allies in the aggression against the Arab peoples. For that reason, any type of playing around with imperialism by any Arab country is dangerous, because political opportunism cannot replace frank, open and revolutionary diplomacy, and sometimes it leads to flagrant betrayal. The present situation in the Middle East is of the deepest concern to the nonaligned countries.

Very important events also took place during 1974.

After ten years of self-sacrificing struggle, the peoples of Guinea-Bissau, Mozambique and Angola brought the fascist, colonial regime of Portugal to the crisis point. As a consequence, revolution erupted in the metropolis itself and the road was opened for the liquidation of Portuguese colonialism in Africa and the liberation of all the peoples it oppressed on that continent. This year will bring with it the official declaration of independence by those peoples still under Portugal's formal domination.

At the same time, it is notable and encouraging for the world progressive movement that the revolutionary process is being deepened and consolidated in Portugal. Until a short time ago the seat of a fascist state which was the instrument of the most obsolete colonialism, opposed and repudiated by world opinion, that country stands today as a revolutionary hope in Western Europe. The Movement of the Nonaligned Countries must greet this historic event with jubilation and firmly support the people and present government of Portugal as new allies in the common cause of liberation and world progress.

In Greece, the fascist military regime allied with NATO and in obvious collusion with the Pentagon, played the principal role in the criminal Cyprus adventure, overthrowing the legitimate government and threatening the independence and integrity of that country which holds a distinguished and honorable position in the Nonaligned Movement. This provoked the immediate reaction of Turkey, another member of NATO, which proceeded to occupy a part of the island militarily.

The irrational adventure and its failure were more than the tottering Greek dictatorship could stand, and unable to resist the sudden reverses in the situation thus created, it fell with a thud. Although this did not produce a revolutionary situation, as in Portugal, an institutional and legal regime has been established in that country and we greet it with satisfaction.

But as a result of the adventures, battles and conflicts among the NATO governments, Cyprus—a nonaligned country—has remained divided de facto by the military intervention of foreign powers, and its integrity is threatened. The Nonaligned Movement cannot be indifferent to this situation without diminishing its prestige. It is necessary that we support the independence and integrity of Cyprus without any hesitation, demanding a solution that takes into account the rights, the collaboration and the understanding of the national minorities involved in the problem.

From the progressive and revolutionary point of view, the events in Ethiopia, which also took place last year, are of great interest and historic importance. That country, which by the way is also a member of the nonaligned family, suffered from a terrible situation of misery and social backwardness. With that situation aggravated by natural calamities, hundreds of thousands of persons have died of hunger in recent years, while an unscrupulous, exploiting class of landowners appropriated up to 80 percent of the production of the peasants. A continuation of that state of affairs would not be in keeping with the times or with the aspirations of today's world. That is why it was inevitable that a revolutionary situation should sooner or later develop in that country. As a revolutionary, I cannot help but rejoice, because I think that not only should the exploitation of some nations by other nations disappear from the world, but also all forms of exploitation of man by man. Unfortunately, a fratricidal struggle between the new government which broke the old structures and a national liberation movement is being waged within that very state. This situation in which two progressive causes are confronting each other is complex. Therefore, what is the duty of the Nonaligned? Is it perhaps to cross our arms or support one side to the detriment of the other? Urge on the war? Decidedly not. The least that should be done is to make a serious effort and seek a peaceful and just solution that would be acceptable to the parties in the conflict which is separating and confronting the Ethiopian revolutionary process and the Liberation Movement of Eritrea. Recently the OPEC worked to seek peace between Iraq and Iran. Why don't the Nonaligned Countries do the same thing in Ethiopia?

In Cambodia, despite United States aid, the usurper regime of Lon Nol is in its death throes. The resolute and heroic struggle of the Cambodian revolutionaries is unrelentingly advancing to a victorious outcome, and nothing can stop it, because this is the inexorable course of events in the world of today.

During this period, we have seen in South Vietnam the outrageous sabotage of the Paris Agreements on the part of the puppet Van Thieu and his Yankee masters. This has prevented that tormented country from enjoying peace and from establishing a democratic and legal regime which would permit the South Vietnamese to decide freely on their form of government and on integration with their brothers and sisters of the North. But the maneuvers of imperialism have been shattered by the resolute and heroic will of the Vietnamese patriots, whose cause is growing stronger day by day while the Saigon regime is deteriorating and nearing the sad end which history reserves for traitors.

The Provisional Revolutionary Government of South Vietnam and the Royal Government of National Union of Cambodia are two states which, by their presence, do honor and bring prestige to the Nonaligned Movement, which should offer them the most energetic and resolute support.

In the international field, the Sixth Special Session of the United Nations General Assembly demonstrated the immense strength which the Nonaligned Movement has today; indeed, every one of the international forums has now turned into a scene of their struggles. Such was the World Food Conference in Rome, and such is the Conference of the United Nations for Industrial Development which is now ending in Lima. Dakar received the representatives of the 77 to establish the program for the defense of fair prices and the markets required for basic products.

The most serious problem which today faces the Nonaligned Countries Movement is the current international economic crisis. This crisis began in the developed capitalist world with galloping inflation, to which has been added a serious economic recession. For the students of Marx, Engels and Lenin, this fact comes as no surprise or mystery. Economic crisis is inherent in the capitalist system, aggravated in this case by the policy of cold war, the arms race and the repression of the national liberation movement which U.S. imperialism fostered after World War II; by unequal trade and the ruthless plunder of the natural resources of the underdeveloped countries of the world by the developed capitalist societies.

The ideologists of imperialism, not taking into account the historically and scientifically proven laws inherent in the system, claimed that capitalism could march forward without limit, without economic crisis; spending, moreover, fabulous sums in armaments; waging unpopular wars such as the one in Vietnam, without bothering to levy taxes for their bellicose purposes; approving deficit budgets; printing paper money and carrying on a superficial waste of resources and a luxury of wealth that are even more insulting when they take place in the midst of a great part of the underdeveloped, hungry world, lacking the most indispensable things, yesterday colonized and subjected by imperialism and today exploited by unequal trade and the ruthless pillage of their raw materials.

Sooner or later, such a policy has to lead to a serious world economic crisis in which, of course, those who suffer are not the bourgeoisie and the financial oligarchs of imperialism nor the feudal lords and wealthy classes that may exist in the underdeveloped world. It is the industrial workers and the humble laborers of city and countryside who bear the brunt of the crisis, especially those in the Third World where poverty and misery are already felt most acutely. Of course, the only real solution to the economic crisis is the disappearance of capitalism from the world. This will happen some day and partially as a result of the crisis. But what concern us are the present-day serious problems in an underdeveloped world which must confront the voracity and the machinations of imperialism, which although in crisis, still has enough powerful economic, technical, political and military resources to try to impose its solutions and shove the burden of the crisis on the shoulders of its own workers and those of the economically backward countries.

This is the challenge facing the Nonaligned Countries Movement and the rest of the underdeveloped world today.

Of course, we, the group of the underdeveloped countries, do not constitute a homogeneous whole. Some oppose imperialism and struggle against it, others in turn are very close to imperialism and in many cases even act as its allies. There is, however, a great range of different situations. That is why it is difficult to draw up a common policy to safeguard the fundamental interests of our peoples, within this essential contradiction between the underdeveloped countries and imperialism. Nonetheless, the Nonaligned Countries Movement has succeeded in uniting a considerable number of countries of different political shades which have demonstrated the possibility of acting together on a series of important questions. It should be affirmed that the future of the underdeveloped world depends largely on the clarity and the decision with which this Movement acts today in solving the economic problems now affecting the underdeveloped world.

Even the unity of the Nonaligned Countries is being put to trial at this moment by imperialism. The issue revolves around the economic crisis and the energy problem. Imperialism seeks to divide the underdeveloped countries into oil-exporting countries and oil-importing countries and, likewise, to split the Nonaligned into countries that export oil and those that import it. And imperialism may succeed if a close unity of interests is not obtained between the oil-producing and non-oil-producing underdeveloped countries.

The facts must be examined objectively.

In the case of the OPEC, for the first time in the history of international relations, a group of underdeveloped countries have managed to set their own trade terms for their basic raw materials vis-á-vis the developed capitalist world. Undoubtedly, we see this as a great victory.

In the same manner, for the first time in history, a relatively small group of underdeveloped countries are accumulating extraordinary amounts of surplus funds formerly under the exclusive control of the developed capitalist countries. This is also a victory, for it opens up new possibilities of resources to the under-developed world.

But oil, among all other raw materials, has a privileged status. Unlike iron, aluminium, zinc, lead, nickel, copper, tin and others which are practically not consumed by the underdeveloped world and which are neither so scarce nor play the role of energy in the developed capitalist world, oil is an essential world commodity. Absolutely no country can do without it. No other raw material of the underdeveloped world could wield the might of oil to demand so big an amendment in the terms of trade.

The developed capitalist countries are transferring a substantial part of the new costs of oil to the underdeveloped world, extraordinarily raising the price of technology, equipment, manufactured and semi-manufactured products, fertilizers, synthetic materials and many others that developing countries must import.

The non-oil-producing underdeveloped world is paying much more for energy, and in 1974 it spent $10 billion more for that purpose.

Furthermore, the non-oil-producing underdeveloped world is paying much more for the technology, equipment and products they import from the developed capitalist world.

Unequal trade for the non-oil-producing underdeveloped countries has become more onerous, for both the industrial products they import from the developed capitalist world and the energy they must import for their subsistence. In short, new unequal trade has emerged for the underdeveloped world.

With few exceptions, the prices for raw materials and products which are essential for a great majority of non-oil-producing countries have been falling considerably in recent months. As a result, while a great number of underdeveloped countries are seeing the prices of their export products reduced, they in turn must pay much more to obtain industrial products and energy. The effect of the world economic crisis is bearing down terribly on them.

On the other hand, surplus funds of approximately $60 billion in the possession of the oil-exporting countries, accumulated in 1974—according to estimates published by capitalist financial sources themselves—were invested as follows: in the European financial market, $21 billion; in the United States, $11 billion; in Great Britain, $8 billion; in public loans issued by developed capitalist countries and direct investments of the oil-producing nations in those countries, more than $10 billion; in international financial institutions, $3.5 billion; and only $2 billion were effectively transferred to underdeveloped countries during this period. That is, while the bulk of these surpluses in one way or another went to the developed capitalist world, the underdeveloped world did not even receive 5 percent of them. It is evident that, except for isolated and individual actions, the oil-producing countries do not have a strategy of economic cooperation with the underdeveloped world, which is basic in order to focus on and to confront, correctly and solidly united, the political and economic risks that the situation implies for all.

Surplus funds gave birth to imperialism. To the extent that the oil-producing countries invest their surplus funds in the developed capitalist world, their interests will inevitably be identified with the interests of imperialism and not with the cause of the exploited peoples of the world. Furthermore, as we have said on another occasion, that capital would serve as a hostage in imperialist hands.

Naturally, financial surpluses must circulate throughout the world's economy, yet the economies of all the countries, including developed countries, can be aided and a crisis of catastrophic dimensions averted only to the extent that a substantial portion of these funds passes through the underdeveloped world and is converted into technology and development.

I am talking about financial surpluses, not resources that the oil-producing countries ought to invest on a priority basis in their own economies. Neither am I talking about donations or gifts, nor direct investments, for that would repeat the history of imperialism, but about credits given under conditions adequate for the development of the countries that need them and provided, of course, that such funds are truly used by those countries for development, for the benefit of their peoples and not in the interest of tiny minorities or foreign monopolies.

This is the policy which we encourage among the Nonaligned Movement and all the other underdeveloped countries.

On September 28 of last year, I said:

"If all the underdeveloped countries are to make the battle of petroleum theirs, it is imperative that the oil-producing countries make the battle of the underdeveloped world theirs."

I know that several oil-producing countries, among them Venezuela, Algeria and Iraq, have shown in various ways their concern about encouraging and defending a correct policy of this type. Others have opened up credit operations for development. At the OPEC summit conference held in Algiers, it was also stated that the oil-exporting countries wanted to work together with the rest of the underdeveloped countries in the struggle against unequal trade terms and in the defense of all the raw-material producers. We salute these initiatives and statements because they are proof of the growing awareness of the seriousness and transcendency of these problems.

Some oil-producing countries, the weakest demographically and militarily, are seriously threatened by imperialist aggression. We do not believe that the statements made by the president of the United States were intended merely to intimidate by threat; we believe they were also intended to pave the way if he should decide to act. I spoke about this danger at the Algiers Summit Conference at a time when the present energy situation had not yet been created. Even before the last Middle East crisis, the United States was training troops for military action in the desert. The present world correlation of forces is far from favorable to imperialism's warmongering ventures, but we must not underestimate the counsel of desperation.

Historical experience shows that the firm union of the peoples and world opinion, plus the will to resist aggression with all energy, are factors that can stop imperialist threats. Cuba has proven it in facing up to these risks and threats 90 miles away from the United States. Our people have victoriously and resolutely resisted the blockade and aggressions thanks to international solidarity and the firm and determined aid of the Soviet Union.

The revolutionary government of Cuba follows a policy of principles in its international conduct. And so at the same time that it is concerned and expresses itself frankly and honestly about the errors that may be committed by the underdeveloped countries themselves, it also reaffirms its determination to close ranks with the Nonaligned Countries, the OPEC countries and the rest of the economically-backward world in order to carry out a united and correct policy in the face of economic crisis, unequal trade terms, plunder of our natural resources, imperialist threats and blackmail. We exhort all the nonaligned countries to work in this direction.

Please forgive me for having spoken extensively. I do not want to conclude without recalling that in many parts of the world other peoples are struggling for their claims and rights against imperialism and reaction. Some I mentioned at the beginning of this address. Others we cannot fail to recall: the people of North Vietnam are devoting themselves to the task of reconstructing their country devastated by the barbarous Yankee bombings. Why not create a fund to help that heroic country which has sacrificed itself so much for the cause of all the peoples of the world? In Korea, a self-sacrificing people bear the country's division imposed by imperialist intervention and presence in the South. In Africa, the odious policy of discrimination, which has been the constant concern of the Nonaligned Countries, continues against numerous peoples and nations. In Latin America, Puerto Rico is awaiting the solidarity of all in its self-sacrificing struggle for liberty; Panama claims its sovereign rights over the usurped Canal territory; Peru carries forward its revolution in the face of imperialist stratagems and conspiracies; Venezuela is nationalizing iron and oil, exploited over decades by foreign monopolies. To all of them we offer our firmest solidarity.

The advances of the liberation movement and the people's victory are encouraging. New and possible conditions have been created for the further advancement of humanity along the roads of justice, liberty, progress and peace.

We are certain that the Nonaligned Countries, closely united with all the progressive forces of the world will know how to live up to what is demanded of us today and in the future.

Many thanks.

The philosophy of plunder and the philosophy of war

Your Excellencies, Guests, Comrades:

I would like to ask that the first moments of this solemn event be dedicated to the memory of a beloved friend whom we all admired, a hero of his country's liberation and revolution, a man who guided the Algiers Summit Conference brilliantly in 1973 and who did much for the strength and prestige of the Nonaligned Movement, the late president of Algeria, Houari Boumedienne. How it grieves us that he cannot be with us in Cuba to share this occasion in our Movement's history. I ask this worthy conference to observe a minute of silence in his memory.

Mr Chairman, Junius Jayawardene, I would like to express my sincere recognition of your constant concern for the future of our Movement and democratic respect for the dissimilar components of this powerful association of countries and the wise prudence you have shown in every difficult situation our nonaligned countries have had to face in the past three years—which have not been easy. In spite of distance and economic problems, your small country has made a noble and worthy effort to live up to the honorable responsibilities entrusted to it in Colombo [Sri Lanka].

I thank all of you for the tremendous honor you do us with your presence here. I greet all of you warmly and welcome you on behalf of our people.

The following speech by Fidel Castro was presented at the inaugural session of the Sixth Summit Conference of the Movement of Nonaligned Countries held in Havana.

'Let the philosophy of plunder cease and the
philosophy of war will cease.'

I would also like to fraternally greet the new countries that are joining our powerful Movement at this Conference: Iran and Pakistan, that become members following the toppling of the Shah's throne and the breaking up of the aggressive, reactionary CENTO military alliance; Surinam; Bolivia; tiny, brave Grenada; and the indomitable people of Nicaragua, whose heroic, self-sacrificing fighters have so recently left the mark of their historic march bringing freedom to Sandino's homeland and dignity to our America.

Ethiopia and Afghanistan now accompany us with a new revolutionary character, and the Patriotic Front of Zimbabwe has full member status.

Our family is growing and increasing in quality, which is the way it should be.

The Philippines, Saint Lucia, Dominica and Costa Rica are new observers and we have a number of guests, including Spain— whose gesture of sending a delegation to this conference for the first time we view as a hope for friendly and useful relations with all the peoples of the world, without allowing itself to be drawn into the aggressive NATO military bloc, which would only serve to compromise and alienate the brilliant future of that self-sacrificing people whose historical, cultural and blood bonds with the nations of our America are so solid. We also need friends in industrialized Western Europe that are not tied to the imperialist wagon.

Ninety-four states and liberation movements are represented here as full members of this Sixth Summit Conference. This Summit Conference is, therefore, the one with the largest attendance and with the greatest number of nonaligned and national liberation movement leaders ever held. This is not something for which our modest country should take credit; rather, it is an unmistakable sign of the vigor, strength and prestige of the Movement of Nonaligned Countries.

All efforts to sabotage the Havana Summit Conference have proved futile. All pressures, hectic diplomatic efforts and intrigues to prevent this conference from being held in our country were in vain.

The Yankee imperialists and their old and new allies—in this case I refer to the Chinese government—didn't want this conference to be held in Cuba.

They also engaged in dirty scheming, saying that Cuba would turn the Movement of Nonaligned Countries into a tool of Soviet policy. We know only too well that the U.S. government even got hold of a copy of the draft final declaration, drawn up by Cuba, and made feverish diplomatic contacts in an effort to modify it. We have irrefutable proof of this.

We believe that the draft—which was submitted to all the member countries earlier than at any other conference and was then redrafted to include many of their suggestions—is a good one but subject to improvement. Improvement means strengthening, not weakening, it. In any case, since when does the United States have the right to involve itself in the Nonaligned Movement and decide how our documents should be drawn up?

What is the reason for the reactionary opposition to Cuba?

Cuba isn't exactly a country that is inconsistent toward the imperialists. Cuba has never ceased to practise a policy of close solidarity with the national liberation movements and all other just causes of our times. Cuba has never hesitated to defend its political principles with determination, energy, dignity, honesty and courage, nor, in over 20 years, has it ever stopped fighting against the aggression and the blockade imposed by the most powerful imperialist country in the world simply because Cuba carried out a genuine political and social revolution just 90 miles from that country's coast.

It is all too well known—and has been admitted and officially published in the United States—that the authorities of that country spent years organizing and methodically plotting to assassinate the leaders of the Cuban revolution, using the most sophisticated means of conspiracy and crime. Nevertheless, in spite of the fact that these deeds were investigated and publicized by the U.S. Senate, the U.S. government has not yet deigned to give any kind of an apology for those vituperative and uncivilized actions.

The true measure of a revolutionary people—the unblemished conduct of a country that cannot be bribed, bought or intimidated—is given by the imperialists' hatred.

In our international relations, we express solidarity with deeds, not fine words. Cuban technicians are now working in 28 countries that belong to our Movement. In the vast majority of those countries, because of their economic limitations, that cooperation is provided without charge, in spite of our own difficulties. Right now, Cuba has twice as many doctors serving abroad as does the UN World Health Organization.

Noble, self-sacrificing Cubans have died thousands of miles from home while supporting liberation movements, defending other peoples' just causes and fighting against the expansionism of the

South African racists and other forms of imperialist attacks on human dignity and the integrity and independence of sister nations. They express the purity, selflessness, solidarity and internationalist consciousness that the revolution has forged among our people.

What charges can be brought against Cuba? That it is a socialist country? Yes, it is a socialist country, but we don't impose our ideology or our system on anyone, either inside or outside the Movement, and being socialist is nothing to be ashamed of. That we had a radical revolution in Cuba? Yes, we are radical revolutionaries, but we don't try to impose our radicalism on anyone, much less on the Nonaligned Movement.

That we maintain fraternal relations with the Soviet Union and the rest of the socialist community? Yes, we are friends of the Soviet Union. We are very grateful to the Soviet people, because their generous cooperation helped us to survive and overcome some very difficult and decisive periods in our people's life, when we were even in danger of being wiped out. No people has the right to be ungrateful. We are grateful to the glorious October Revolution because it ushered in a new era in human history, made it possible to defeat fascism and created a world situation in which the peoples' self-sacrificing struggle led to the downfall of the hateful colonial system. To ignore that is to ignore history itself.

Not only Cuba but also Vietnam, the Arab countries under attack; the peoples in the former Portuguese colonies; the revolutionary processes in many other countries throughout the world; and the liberation movements that fight against oppression, racism, Zionism and fascism in South Africa, Namibia, Zimbabwe, Palestine and elsewhere owe a debt of gratitude to socialist solidarity. I wonder whether the United States or any other NATO country has ever helped a single liberation movement anywhere in the world. In fact, I am convinced—and I have said so on other occasions—that, without the power and influence which the socialist community exerts today imperialism, harassed by the economic crisis and by the shortage of basic raw materials, would not hesitate to divide up the world again. It has already done so more than once. It is even theatening to do so again and, in point of fact, is creating special intervention forces aimed menacingly at the oil-exporting countries. To cite just one example of this, the United States has unilaterally decided to respect no more than a three-mile limit of maritime sovereignty.

If membership in the Nonaligned Movement depended on betraying our deepest ideas and convictions, it would not be honorable for me or for any of you to belong to it. No revolutionary has the right to be a coward.

There are some who have made an art of opportunism. We Cuban revolutionaries are not and never will be opportunists. We know how to sacrifice our own national economic interests whenever necessary to defend a just principle or an honorable political position. We Cubans will never renege on what we said yesterday, nor will we say one thing today and do something else tomorrow.

We are firmly anti-imperialist, anticolonial, antineocolonial, anti-racist, anti-Zionist and antifascist, because these principles are a part of our thinking; they constitute the essence and origin of the Movement of Nonaligned Countries and have formed its life and history ever since its founding. These principles are also very fresh in the life and history of the peoples we represent here.

Was any country that now belongs to our Movement really independent more than 35 years ago? Is there any member that hasn't known colonialism, neocolonialism, fascism, racial discrimination or imperialist aggression; economic dependency; poverty; squalor; illiteracy; and the most brutal exploitation of its natural and human resources? What country doesn't bear the burden of the technological gap, a lower standard of living than the former metropolises, unequal terms of trade, the economic crisis, inflation and underdevelopment imposed on our peoples by centuries of colonial exploitation and imperialist domination?

Cuba will be in the front line defending these principles with independence and the unique, prestigious, fraternal and ever more constructive and influential role of the Nonaligned Movement in international life, so the energetic and rightful voice of our peoples may be heard.

Moreover, I believe that, if you thought Cuba had no position of its own, was not completely independent or lacked the loyalty and honesty it owes the Movement in line with its concepts and goals, you would not have given your generous cooperation, confidence, interest and enthusiasm to this Sixth Summit Conference.

Throughout our revolutionary life, no one has ever tried to tell us what to do. No one has ever tried to tell us what role we should play in the Movement of Nonaligned Countries. No one told us when or how to make the revolution in our country, nor could anyone have done so. By the same token, no one except the Movement itself can determine what it should do and when and how to do it.

We have worked tirelessly to create the material and political

24

conditions to make this event a success. We have respected and we will continue to totally respect the rights of all members of the Movement. We have fully and scrupulously fulfilled our duties as host country and will continue to do so. Our views will not always coincide with those of each and every one of you. We have many close friends at this conference, but we don't always agree with the best of them. We hope that everyone will speak out with the greatest freedom and honesty and feel that he is being heard with interest, respect and consideration. The combined experiences of all of us gathered here can produce tremendous results. Certain topics are controversial, and certain words may seem strong. If anything we say displeases anyone, please understand that we do not mean to hurt or wound. We will work with all member countries—without exception—to achieve our aims and to implement the agreements that are adopted. We will be patient, prudent, flexible, calm. Cuba will observe these norms throughout the years in which it presides over the Movement. I declare this categorically.

We have grown and advanced. Fortunately, Mozambique, Angola, São Tomé and Principe, Guinea-Bissau and the Cape Verde Islands are now fully independent countries, after a heroic and unequal struggle. Today, as sovereign states, they are prestigious and influential members of our Movement. Just six years ago, at the Algiers Summit Conference, they were only liberation movements.

Vietnam is united and free after 30 years of extraordinary and admirable struggle.

The Shah is no longer the Shah. CENTO no longer exists; Somoza is no longer in power; and the fascist Gairy no longer rules tiny, heroic Grenada. These are unquestionable victories for independence, progress and freedom. Our causes triumph because they are just!

Growing numbers of peoples are joining our ranks as they break the bonds of colonialism, neocolonialism, fascism and other forms of oppression and dependency. In one way or another, all these struggles have been supported by the Movement of Nonaligned Countries, and these are victories for us, as well.

Nevertheless, imperialism has not ceased its tenacious efforts to maintain its subjection, oppression and occupation of other peoples and countries, whose causes demand our resolute support.

First of all, I refer to the long-suffering, courageous Palestinian people. No more brutal pillage of a people's rights to peace and existence has occurred in this century. Please understand that we are not fanatics. The revolutionary movement has always learned to hate racial discrimination and pogroms of any kind. From the bottom of our heart, we repudiate the merciless persecution and genocide that the Nazis once visited on the Jews, but there's nothing in recent history that parallels it more that the dispossession, persecution and genocide that imperialism and Zionism are currently practicing against the Palestinian people. Pushed off their lands, expelled from their own country, scattered throughout the world, persecuted and murdered, the heroic Palestinians are a vivid example of sacrifice and patriotism, living symbols of the most terrible crime of our era.

Piece by piece, Palestinian lands and the territories of neighboring Arab countries—Syria, Jordan and Egypt—have been seized by the aggressors, armed to the teeth with the most sophisticated weapons from the U.S. arsenal.

The just Palestinian and Arab cause has been supported by world progressive opinion and our Movement for nearly 20 years. Nasser was one of the prestigious founders of this Movement. Nevertheless, all UN resolutions have been scornfully ignored and rejected by the aggressors and their imperialist allies.

Imperialism has sought to impose its own peace, using betrayal and division. An armed, dirty, unjust, bloody peace will never be a true peace.

The Camp David agreement is a flagrant betrayal of the Arab cause and of the Palestinian, Lebanese, Syrian, Jordanian—all the Arab peoples, including the Egyptians, It is a betrayal of all the progressive peoples of the world who, at the United Nations and all other international forums, have always supported a just solution to the problem of the Middle East, one that would be acceptable and honorable for all and guaranteed by all.

True peace in the Middle East can never be built on such injustice, such a Machiavellian policy, such betrayal and such flimsy bases.

Instead of one gendarme for the Middle East, the Arab world and Africa, imperialism now wants two: Israel and Egypt. If peace really exists between Egypt and Israel, why does Egypt need all the weapons it is getting—even though they aren't as sophisticated and modern as the ones that are going to the Israelis? How will these arms be used, except against the peoples in the area, including the Egyptians themselves?

International policy should be ethical. The Movement of Nonaligned Countries should roundly denounce the Camp David agreement. Moral censure, at least, is essential.

We have witnessed ten years of imperialist maneuvers, deceit and crimes in Zimbabwe. Six million Africans there are oppressed by a tiny, arrogant and genocidal racist, fascist minority. We should firmly denounce and reject the so-called internal settlement and Muzorewa's puppet regime, which is a mockery of Africa's conscience, and give the Patriotic Front of Zimbabwe—sole legitimate representative of its people—the Nonaligned Movement's all-out support and solidarity.

The people of Namibia are also suffering from South Africa's scorn, mockery and disrespect for United Nations' orders and resolutions—and South Africa is fully supported by the NATO powers, including the United States. Racist South African troops that have no right to be there are depriving the Namibian people of their independence and imposing a bantustan system on that long-suffering country, in defiance of the international community and world public opinion.

South Africa itself constitutes the most shameful blot for the peoples of Africa and the world. Human dignity cannot help but be offended by that repulsive stronghold of the Nazi-fascist spirit that remains in the Southern Cone of Africa, where 20 million Africans are oppressed, exploited, discriminated against and repressed by a handful of racists. Who spawned that system? Who supports it? They say the South African racists even know how to make atom bombs. Against whom are they likely to be used? Against the black ghettos of Pretoria? Will they, perchance, be used to block the just and inevitable liberation of the people?

Why are the Rhodesian and South African racists allowed to bomb Mozambique, Zambia, Angola and Botswana almost daily, murdering with impunity thousands upon thousands of refugees and citizens of those countries, as well? Why are the Zionist aggressors permitted to bomb the Palestinian refugee camps and Lebanese towns daily? Who has given them that right? Who has given them that power? Why are they allowed to use the most sophisticated weapons of destruction and death? Who supplies them? Isn't this undeniable proof of imperialism's aggressive role and the type of peace and order it wants for our people? Or isn't it a crime to kill a child, an old man, a woman, a black adult, a Palestinian, a Lebanese? Can these methods and these concepts be differentiated from the methods and concepts that fascist Germany once used? Reports of genocidal acts of this nature are broadcast daily, even by the imperialist press agencies, as if to accustom us to accepting such deeds with resignation and meekness.

Another problem that concerns African and world opinion is that of Western Sahara. Cuba has no particular dispute with Morocco, whose government maintained diplomatic and trade relations with us even in the most critical period of the U.S. blockade of our country. But looking at the matter from a principled point of view, Cuba expresses its total support for the independence of the Saharan people, considering the occupation of their territory to be utterly unfounded and their desire for free self-determination to be unquestionably just. Cuba was a member of the UN commission that investigated the desires of the Saharan people prior to the conflict and can attest to the fact that 99 percent of the inhabitants want independence. We congratulate Mauritania on its courageous decision to renounce all territorial claims and hope that Morocco will reconsider its policy on Western Sahara, a policy that not only isolates and weakens its international position but also exhausts and impoverishes it economically. The right to independence of the valiant Saharan people and the Polisario Front, their legitimate representative, should be recognized by all.

We support the people of Cyprus in their struggle against the foreign occupation of a part of their territory and for the development of peace and fraternal coexistence by all components of that sister country's population.

Cuba's position on the problems in Southeast Asia is crystal clear. For our people, Vietnam is sacred. We once swore that we were willing to die for Vietnam.

No other people of recent times has paid such a high price in sacrifice, suffering and death in order to be free; no people has made a greater contribution to the national liberation struggle; no other people has done so much in this period to create a universal anti-imperialist consciousness. Four times as many bombs were dropped on Vietnam as were used in World War II; the most powerful imperialist country had its claws cut off in Vietnam; Vietnam taught all oppressed nations that no force can defeat a people that is determined to fight for its freedom. The struggle in Vietnam reinforced the respect and dignity of all our peoples.

Now, when Vietnam has been made the victim of intrigue, slander and encirclement by the Yankee imperialists and of betrayal, conspiracy and aggression by the government of China, Cuba offers it its firmest support.

With all their talk about the problem of the Vietnamese refugees —who are the direct result of colonialism, underdevelopment and the 30-year war of aggression—why don't the U.S. government and its allies even mention the millions of Palestinians scattered all over the world and the hundreds of thousands of Zimbabwean, Namibian and South African refugees who are dispersed, persecuted and murdered in Africa?

What right does China have to teach Vietnam a lesson, invade its territory, destroy its modest wealth and murder thousands of its people? The Chinese ruling clique, that supported Pinochet against Allende, that supported South Africa's aggression against Angola, that supported the Shah, that supported Somoza, that supports and supplies weapons to Sadat, that justifies the Yankee blockade against Cuba and the continued existence of the naval base at Guantánamo, that defends NATO and sides with the United States and the most reactionary forces of Europe and the rest of the world, has neither the prestige nor the moral standing to teach anybody a lesson.

We also support the Lao People's Republic against the Chinese government's threats of aggression and expansionism.

Cuba's position on the problem of Kampuchea is known. We recognize the only real, legitimate government of Kampuchea, which is the People's Revolutionary Council of the People's Republic of Kampuchea, and we endorse Vietnam's solidarity with that fraternal country. People keep saying that Vietnam sent fighters to support the Kampuchean revolutionaries. Why don't they say that the bloody clique that had seized control of the country, in complicity with China and imperialism, provoked and attacked Vietnam first and that there is indisputable documentary proof of mass murders perpetrated against Vietnamese men, women, old people and children?

With all our energy, we condemn the genocidal government of Pol Pot and Ieng Sary. Three million dead accuse them. Even Sihanouk has admitted that some of his relatives were murdered. It is a shameful thing for the progressive forces of the world that such crimes could ever have been committed in the name of the revolution and socialism.

Nevertheless, Cuba, mindful of its obligations as host country, offered the facilities for both parties to be present in Havana until the Movement comes to a decision in this regard. It is inexplicable that, while some oppose the expulsion of Egypt, that allied itself with the United States and Israel, openly betraying the noble Arab cause and the Palestinian people, efforts are being made to condemn Vietnam for its acts of legitimate defense against aggression and the fiction is maintained that Pol Pot's bloody government, an affront to all humanity, still exists.

The Movement should preserve its unity and always seek a peaceful solution to any difference that may arise among its members, but it is equally bound to maintain impartiality, realism and political logic in its decisions. Tanzania was also obliged to defend itself against Uganda's aggression and to support the patriots of that country against the repressive regime. Now, the legitimate, revolutionary government of Uganda is represented in this conference. Why should we deny this right to People's Kampuchea?

We firmly support the Korean people's struggle for the reunification of their country. We denounce the unjust division and virtual occupation of a part of their territory by U.S. troops. We denounce the inconsistency and hollowness of the U.S. government's promises, because, far from reducing those troops, it is reinforcing them and increasing their aggressive potential.

In our America, we reiterate our firm and staunch solidarity with the fraternal people of Puerto Rico, whose right to self-determination and independence is stubbornly denied by the colonizing power. Puerto Rico—just like Zimbabwe, Namibia, South Africa, Palestine and other countries—needs our help, and we must give it unhesitatingly and unswervingly, in spite of the strong pressures that the United States constantly brings to bear on all countries in this regard.

We support Panama's right to full sovereignty over the Canal and condemn the reactionary maneuvers aimed at hindering implementation of the new treaty.

We support Belize's right to independence, which is being held back mainly by the opposition and threats of the bloody, pro-Yankee satrap who oppresses Guatemala. The people of Belize are completely different from the people of Guatemala—ethnically, culturally and historically—and both of them need freedom equally.

The new Nicaragua requires maximum cooperation from the international community for the reconstruction of the country, which was destroyed by nearly half a century of the Somoza dynasty, spawned by the Yankee Marines. It is only right that we give it our solidarity.

Bolivia, whose territories were cut up a century ago in a war promoted by imperialist interests, aspires to have an outlet to the sea, and this is absolutely justified and vital. We therefore consider it our duty to support it.

We are opposed to the continued existence of any kind of colonial enclave in this hemisphere.

Cuba needs solidarity, too. Our country is suffering from a criminal, savage economic blockade imposed by the United States—a blockade which is even applied against medicines—and a part of our national territory is still occupied by force.

Does the United States have the right to try to prevent our development at all costs? Does it have the right to own military bases in another country against the will of its people?

All these topics and struggles about which we are concerned and that require our solidarity contain a constant, invariable element: the action of imperialism. Can our Movement ignore it? Is it, perhaps, extremism on our part to set forth the facts clearly?

Even though the underdeveloped countries, which suffer from poverty and very low living standards and life expectancies, have the least to lose in a war, we cannot be insensitive to the need for world peace. If we were, it would mean giving up hopes of better future for the peoples. We do not support the thesis that a world nuclear war is inevitable. That fatalistic, irresponsible attitude is the surest path to the annihilation of humanity in a universal holocaust. Never before has humanity had that technological possibility. We cannot be so stupid as to ignore it. For the first time in history our generation has had to confront these risks.

In our world today, mountains of ever more deadly weapons are piling up, along with mountains of problems of underdevelopment, poverty, food shortages, squalor, environmental pollution, school and housing shortages, unemployment and an explosive population growth. Such natural resources as land, water, energy and raw materials are beginning to be in short supply in various parts of the world.

The developed capitalist societies not only created wasteful and untenable models for standards of living and consumption but also, unfortunately, propagated them throughout a large part of the world. Many countries in our area conceive of development only as the aspiration to get to be and live like New York, London or Paris.

One way or another, the world economic crisis, the energy crisis, inflation, depression and unemployment oppress the peoples and governments of a large part of the earth. Very few, if any, of the members of our Movement are free of these difficulties, because we bear the brunt of these calamities.

The struggle for peace and for a just economic order and a workable solution to the pressing problems that weigh on our peoples is, in our opinion, increasingly becoming the main question posed to the Movement of Nonaligned Countries.

Peace, with the immense risks that threaten it, is not something that should be left exclusively in the hands of the big military powers. Peace is possible, but world peace can only be assured to the extent that all countries are consciously determined to fight for it—peace not just for a part of the world, but for all peoples. Peace, also, for Vietnam; the Palestinians; the patriots of Zimbabwe and Namibia; the oppressed majorities in South Africa; Angola; Zambia; Mozambique; Botswana; Ethiopia; Syria; Lebanon; and the Saharan people. Peace with justice, peace with independence, peace with freedom. Peace for the powerful countries. Peace for all continents and all peoples. We understand perfectly well that we will not achieve it without a tenacious, resolute struggle, but we should believe in the possibility of achieving it in spite of imperialism. neocolonialism, racism, Zionism, expansionism and the other regressive elements that still exist in the world. The united strength of our countries is very great. Never before have the forces of progress and the advanced political awareness of the peoples attained such high levels. Even within the imperialist, reactionary countries themselves, important progressive sectors are determined to struggle for the same ends. The important role that the people of the United States and world opinion played in ending the criminal imperialist war against Vietnam should never be forgotten.

We must demand peace, détente, peaceful coexistence and disarmament. We must demand and win them, because they will not come about by spontaneous generation, and there is no alternative in today's world, if we are to preserve the very existence of humanity.

We must encourage every step that leads along this path. Therefore, we should welcome the SALT II agreements between the Soviet Union and the United States and the future steps that are promised in this field. At the same time, we should denounce the reactionary forces that support the cold war and that, mixed up in the dirty business of arms sales, destruction and death, oppose the ratification of these agreements in the U.S. Senate.

We realize, however, that although these steps are positive and important, they are still far from the ideal of denuclearization that continues until all nuclear weapons have disappeared—which, in the end, would be the only fair and equal state of affairs for all nations and would mean the end of the arms race. The day should come when humanity resolutely condemns arms production and trade.

More than $300 billion a year is spent on arms and other military expenditures throughout the world, according to statistical publications, and this figure may be a conservative one. The U.S. military forces alone, for example, use 30 million tons of oil for these purposes—more than all the energy used by all the countries in Central America and the Caribbean put together.

This $300 billion could build 600,000 schools, with a capacity for 400 million children; or 60 million comfortable homes, for 300 million people; or 30,000 hospitals, with 18 million beds; or 20,000 factories, with jobs for more that 20 million workers; or an irrigation system for 150 million hectares of land—that, with the application of technology, could feed a billion people. Humanity wastes this much every year on military spending. Moreover, consider the enormous quantites of young human resources, scientific resources, technicians, fuel, raw materials and other items. This is the fabulous price of preventing a true climate of confidence and peace from existing in the world.

We Marxists consider war and weapons to be historically and inevitably tied to the system of man's exploitation of man and to that system's insatiable greed in seizing the natural resources of other peoples. Once, in the United Nations, I said, "Put an end to the philosophy of plunder, and the philosopy of war will be ended."

Socialism does not need arms production to keep its economy going. It doesn't need armies whose purpose is to seize the resources of other peoples. If the slogan of unity and fraternity among all peoples and men reflected today's reality, there would be no need for arms either to attack and oppress people or to win freedom and defend it.

No matter how long or utopian the path may seem and no matter how harsh the setbacks and even betrayals within the progressive movement, we should never become discouraged or stop persevering in our struggle to attain these objectives. It is absolutely necessary to demand in all international forums and organizations that we move from rhetoric to deeds.

These questions lead us directly to the topic of economics. More and more statesmen and leaders in our Movement are stating the need to place this matter at the center of our concerns. You are statesmen who wrestle every day with the knotty economic questions of your countries. You know full well what the great difficulties are: the constantly rising foreign debt, a shortage of foreign currency, the soaring prices of fuel and other import products, unequal terms of trade, low prices on the foreign market that constantly and increasingly rob us of the products that are the fruit of our peoples' labor, inflation, the rise of domestic prices and all the social conflicts that arise from this state of affairs.

Progressive governments that are making a noble effort to develop and increase the well-being of their countries are overwhelmed and may even be wiped out by economic difficulties and unfair, unpopular conditions imposed by the international credit agencies. What political price haven't many of you had to pay because of the rules laid down by the International Monetary Fund? We Cubans, who were excluded from that institution because of an imperialist dictate, aren't quite sure whether that exclusion was a punishment or a privilege.

Some governments placed in power by the people's revolutionary struggle suddenly find themselves faced with horrifying conditions of poverty, indebtedness and underdevelopment that prevent them from responding to even the most modest hopes of their peoples.

I'm not going to tell you half-truths, nor am I going to hide the fact that social difficulties are much greater when, in any of our countries, a small minority controls the basic wealth and the majority of the people are completely dispossessed. In short, if the system is socially just, the possibilities of survival and economic and social development are incomparably greater. Some countries present the phenomenon of growing economies with equally growing poverty, illiteracy, the number of children who have no schools to go to, malnutrition, disease, begging and unemployment—all of which show in no uncertain terms that something is wrong.

The underdeveloped countries—some optimistically prefer to call them developing countries, when, in fact, the gap separating their per capita incomes and standards of living from those of the developed countries is constantly widening—contain 65 percent of the world's population but account for only 15 percent of total world production and only 8 percent of industrial production. The conglomerate of countries in this category, which have no natural energy sources, now have a foreign debt of over $300 billion. It is estimated that around $40 billion a year goes to servicing this foreign debt—more than 20 percent of their exports. Average per capita income in the developed countries is now 14 times greater than in the underdeveloped countries. In addition, the underdeveloped countries contain more than 900 million illiterate adults. This situation is untenable.

One of the most acute problems facing the non-oil producing underdeveloped countries—the vast majority of the members of our Movement—is the energy crisis. The oil-exporting countries —all of which are in the underdeveloped world and almost all of which belong to the Movement of Nonaligned Countries—have always been supported by the rest of our countries in their just demands for the revaluation of their product and an end to unequal terms of trade and the wasting of energy. These countries now have a much greater economic potential and negotiating capacity with the developed capitalist world. This is not the case of the non-oil-producing underdeveloped countries. Sugar, bauxite, copper and other solid minerals, peanuts, copra, sisal, tea, cashews and agricultural products in general are terribly underpriced on the world market. The developed capitalist countries selfishly raise their tariffs against those few products that our countries manufacture and even subsidize goods that compete with ours, whenever possible. The European Economic Community and the United States do this, for example, with sugar. The prices of the equipment, machinery, industrial articles and semifinished products that we import are raised constantly; the privileged exporters of these goods charge ever higher prices for them. It is easier for them than for the underdeveloped countries to pay for fuel. They even export tens of billions of dollars' worth of arms annually and often buy oil with this money. The Shah of Iran was one of their favorite multimillionaire clients, until he was rightly overthrown not long ago. Most of the surplus money from oil sales is deposited and invested in the richest, most developed capitalist countries. These funds are also used to supply them with fuel. But what recourse do the non-oil-producing underdeveloped countries have?

It is absolutely necessary to be aware of this reality, because the situation of many countries, a large number of which are members of this Movement, is truly desperate. We should consider and discuss this matter. A solution must be found. Imperialism is already maneuvering to divide us; it is trying to isolate the oil-producing countries from the rest of the underdeveloped world, blaming them for the economic crisis—whose cause really lies in the unjust order established in the world by the imperialist system. And, what is even more dangerous, it is looking for

35

pretexts and covering up its aggressive plans against the oil-exporting countries.

Cuba isn't bringing this topic up in order to defend interests that affect it directly. Of course, we suffer from the indirect effects of the international economic crisis and the low prices established for our products in Western markets, but we have an assured supply of oil which we purchase with sugar, whose price is directly proportional to the price of oil and other articles which we import from the socialist area.

Nevertheless, we should point out that if all the sugar produced in Cuba—nearly 8 million tons in the 1979 harvest, the largest production of cane sugar in the world—had been sold to the Western world at the price now being paid on the so-called world market—around 8 cents a pound—it wouldn't have paid for the fuel that Cuba uses, at its present price.

We must look for solutions to the energy crisis, but not only for the developed countries, that already use most of the energy produced in the world. We must also find solutions for the underdeveloped countries.

We appeal to the sense of responsibility of the large oil-exporting countries in our Movement, asking them to strike out courageously, firmly and boldly in implementing a wise and farsighted policy of economic cooperation, supplies and investments in our underdeveloped world, because their future depends on ours.

I am not asking you to sacrifice your legitimate interests. I am not asking you to stop all-out efforts to develop and raise the well-being of your own peoples. I am not asking you to stop trying to safeguard your future. I am inviting you to join us and to close ranks with us and struggle together for a real new international economic order whose benefits will extend to all.

No money can purchase the future, because the future lies in justice, in our consciences and in the honest and fraternal solidarity of our peoples.

The solution to the economic problems faced by our countries requires a tremendous, responsible, conscious and serious effort of a world nature.

Those of us meeting here represent the vast majority of the peoples of the world. Let us close ranks and unite the growing forces of our vigorous Movement in the United Nations and in all other international forums to demand economic justice for our peoples and an end to foreign control over our resources and the theft of our labor. Let us close ranks in demanding respect for our right to development, to life and to the future. Enough of building a world economy based on the opulence of those who exploited and impoverished us in the past and who exploit and impoverish us today. Enough of poverty, the economic and social underdevelopment, of the vast majority of humanity. May a firm determination to struggle and concrete plans of action come out of this Sixth Summit Conference: deeds, not just words.

Perhaps this speech inaugurating this conference has been somewhat undiplomatic, not quite in line with protocol, but no one should doubt the complete loyalty with which I have spoken.

Thank you.

'With $300 billion you could in one year build
600,000 schools with a capacity for 400 million
children; 60 million comfortable homes for 300
million people; 30,000 hospitals with 18 million
beds; 20,000 factories with jobs for more than 20
million workers; or build irrigation systems to
water 150 million hectares of land, which with
appropriate technology could feed a billion
people. Humanity wastes this much every year on
its military spending.'

Our Movement is more united, powerful and independent

Dear Friends:

I am not going to give a speech. After 27 hours of continuous activity without a second's rest, after more than 20 hours of sessions, I am not sure I could put together a sensible speech.

Furthermore, everything that can be said has already been said—and better than I could say it. I am sure you would all like me to be brief.

It has been said that this has been the largest meeting of heads of state and other leaders ever held. It may well be the first time a group of responsible men, statesmen, have been in a plenary session from eight in the evening to nine in the morning. Probably never before at an international conference have people worked as hard as we have worked here.

Ninety-three statesmen have spoken from this rostrum, and this doesn't include today's speakers. Truly brilliant, talented, extraordinary men have participated in the debate. As I watched them, I thought of all the human worth in our world; of how many fine figures have emerged; and of how many leaders there are of high quality, seriousness, honesty, commitment to struggle and enthu-

As the new chairman of the Movement of Nonaligned Countries, Fidel Castro gave the following speech at the closing session of the Sixth Summit Conference held in Havana, Cuba. The speech was given on 9 September 1979.

siasm. Without any exaggeration, we would say that many of our world's finest leaders have spoken, debated and worked together during these past few days.

I have thought how useful it would be to gather together all the speeches and publish them in a book to be sent to all the participants in this conference. I, myself, plan to reread, analyze and meditate on everything that has been said here, and I am certain that no other book would be richer in experiences or give us more information or a more accurate assessment of our world's problems.

At this conference the spirit of solidarity has shone as never before. At this conference we have analyzed the most important, the most urgent problems of our time. There has not been one single just cause, one single hope of our peoples, that has not been fully considered and supported at this conference. At this conference we have spoken as never before of the problems of peace. At this conference we have spoken as never before of economic problems, and it was rightly said that economic problems should be at the heart of our concerns and our work.

Toward the end of the Summit Conference, a resolution was proposed expressing our members' concern for carrying out practical, concrete tasks. I am glad that, at the end of the conference, we did not precipitously adopt a resolution on problems that need attention, thought, analysis and the utmost seriousness. The fact that we did not adopt the proposed resolution does not mean that we are postponing to the next conference—or indefinitely—the discussion and adoption of concrete decisions we should have made in this sphere.

A very important—perhaps the most important—aspect of this conference was that, while our enemies predicted that there would be a split and that the Sixth Summit Conference of the Movement of Nonaligned Countries would go off like a grenade (they were counting on what has been said over and over again—that ours is a heterogeneous movement of countries—and on the serious pitfalls we faced), we have survived the pitfalls, tackled the most difficult problems and adopted agreements on each of them through nearly unanimous consensus. Therefore, we can say that our Movement is more united than ever, more vigorous than ever, more powerful than ever, more independent than ever and more ours than ever.

From the responsible positions that correspond to our country, we will do everything we can to carry out the Movement's agreements and strengthen its unity, because, in spite of our differences, we have seen how many interests and goals we have in common.

This conference gave us the opporutnity to see how close we are, how equal we are and that we are all brothers.

Someone said here tonight that, in a few hours, when we had all gone, this room would be very empty, but we are going to feel even emptier inside when all of you leave.

I have been so absorbed in the work of the conference that sometimes, when I was sitting in that chair, I forgot I was in my own country and felt as if I were off attending a conference in some other country.

Really, it has been a memorable experience.

I cannot find the words to thank all of you, to thank all of you for the support you have given the conference — which, in a way, was also support for my country. Impossible to convey how honoured we have been to have you here. Impossible to tell you how encouraging and stimulating your attendance has been, in spite of distance — in spite of the thousands of miles that must be traveled in order to come to our country from Africa, Europe, Asia and Latin America. It is impossible to tell you how deeply we appreciate the fact that, in spite of all the slander campaigns and dire predictions, you did not hesitate to participate in this conference. It is impossible to tell you how deeply we treasure the proof of friendship, solidarity and support that so many of you have given us.

How much it inspires us to keep on struggling, fighting and practicing solidarity and internationalism, because it is what is done for others, for other peoples, for humanity, that gives meaning to a revolutionary's life and makes us feel members of the human family.

This conference has given our country great prestige and great authority, but they will never be used for our country's benefit. We will use them to struggle and work for others. Cuba will not use the leadership position it will have in the Movement for the next few years for its own benefit.

One thing we can say: Cuba will make more sacrifices and will work harder than ever for others.

It is not my place to say that the Sixth Summit Conference has been a success. Let history be the judge of that.

I declare the Sixth Summit Conference of the Movement of Nonaligned Countries closed.

Thank you very much.

'Bombs may kill the hungry, the sick and the ignorant, but bombs cannot kill hunger, disease and ignorance. Nor can bombs kill the righteous rebellion of the peoples.'

We represent the great majority of humanity

Most Esteemed President; Distinguished representatives of the world community:

I have not come to speak about Cuba. I am not here to denounce before this Assembly the aggressions to which our small but honorable country has been subjected for 20 years. Nor have I come to injure with unneccessary adjectives the powerful neighbor in his own house.

We have been charged by the Sixth Conference of heads of state or government of the Movement of Nonaligned Countries to present to the United Nations the results of its deliberations and the positions to be derived from them.

We are 95 countries from all the continents, representing the great majority of humanity. We are united by the determination to defend the cooperation between our countries, free national and social development, sovereignty, security, equality, and self-determination.

We are associated in our determination to change the present system of international relations, based as it is on injustice, inequality, and oppression. In international politics we act as an independent world factor.

Meeting in Havana, the Movement has just reaffirmed its principles and confirmed its objectives.

As the new chairman of the Movement of Nonaligned Countries, Fidel Castro gave the following speech to a meeting of the United Nations General Assembly on 12 October 1979.

The nonaligned countries stress that it is imperative to do away with the enormous inequality that separates the developed countries from the developing countries. We are struggling to eradicate poverty, hunger, disease, and illiteracy, from which hundreds of millions of human beings still suffer.

We aspire to a new world order, one based on justice, on equity, and on peace. One that will replace the unjust and unequal system that prevails today, in which, as proclaimed in the final declaration of Havana, "wealth is still concentrated in the hands of a few powers, whose wasteful economies are maintained by the exploitation of the workers as well as the transfer and plunder of the natural and other resources of the peoples of Africa, Latin America, Asia, and other regions of the world."

Among the problems to be debated in the present session of the General Assembly, peace is a concern of the first order. The search for peace also constitutes an aspiration of the Movement of Nonaligned Countries and has been the subject of its attention at the Sixth Conference. But for our countries, peace is indivisible. We want a peace that will equally benefit the large and small, the strong and weak, peace that will embrace all regions of the world and reach all its citizens.

Since its very inception of the Movement of Nonaligned Countries has considered that the principles of peaceful coexistence should be the cornerstone of international relations, constituting the basis for the strengthening of peace and international security, for the relaxation of tensions and the expansion of that process to all regions of the world and to all aspects of international relations, and must be universally applied in relations among states.

But, at the same time, the Sixth Summit Conference considered that these principles of peaceful coexistence also include the right of peoples under alien and colonial domination to self-determination, to independence, sovereignty, the territorial integrity of states, the right of every country to put an end to foreign occupation, to the acquisition of territory by force, and the right to choose its own social, economic, and political system.

Only in this way can peaceful coexistence be the foundation for all international relations.

And this cannot be denied. When we analyze the structure of the world today, we see that these rights of our peoples are as yet not guaranteed. The nonaligned countries know full well who our historic enemies are, where the threats come from, and how to combat them.

That is why in Havana we resolved to reaffirm that "the quintessence of the policy of nonalignment, in accordance with its original principles and essential character, involves the struggle against imperialism, colonialism and neocolonialism, apartheid, racism, including Zionism, and all forms of foreign aggression, occupation, domination, interference, or hegemony as well as the struggle against great power and bloc policies."

Thus it will be understood that the final declaration of Havana also linked the struggle for peace with "political, moral, and material support for the national liberation movements and joint efforts to eliminate colonial domination and racial discrimination."

The nonaligned countries have always attached great importance to the possibility and necessity of détente among the great powers. Thus the Sixth Conference pointed with great concern to the fact that in the period that elapsed after the Colombo summit conference [of 1976] there was a certain stagnation in the process of détente, which has continued to be limited "both in scope and geographically."

On the basis of that concern the nonaligned countries—who have made disarmament and denuclearization one of the permanent and most prominent objectives of their struggle, and who took the initiative in convening the tenth special session of the General Assembly on disarmament—examined the results of negotiations on strategic arms and the agreements known as SALT II. They feel that those negotiations constitute an important step in the negotiations between the two main nuclear powers and could open up prospects for more comprehensive negotiations leading to general disarmament and relaxation of international tensions.

But as far as the nonaligned countries are concerned, those treaties are only part of the progress toward peace. Although negotiations between the great powers constitute a decisive element in the process, the nonaligned countries once again reiterated that the endeavor to consolidate détente, to extend it to all parts of the world, and to avert the nuclear threat, the arms build up, and war is a task in which all the peoples of the world should participate and exercise their responsibility.

Mr President, basing ourselves on the concept of the universality of peace, and on the need to link the search for peace, extended to all countries, with the struggle for national independence, full sovereignty, and full equality among states, we, the heads of state or government who met at the Sixth Summit Conference in Havana, gave our attention to the most pressing problems in Africa, Asia, Latin America, and other regions.

It is important to stress that we started from an independent position that was not linked to policies that might stem from the contradiction between the great powers. If in spite of that objective and uncommitted approach, our review of international events became a denunciation of the supporters of imperialism and colonialism, this merely reflects the essential reality of today's world.

Thus, having started the analysis of the situation in Africa, and having recognized the progress made in the African peoples' struggle for their emancipation, the heads of state or government stressed that a fundamental problem of the region is the need to eliminate from the continent, and especially from southern Africa, colonialism, racism, racial discrimination, and apartheid.

It was indispensable to stress the fact that the colonialist and imperialist powers were continuing their aggressive policies with the aim of perpetuating, regaining, or extending their domination and exploitation of the African nations.

This is precisely the dramatic situation in Africa. The nonaligned countries could not fail to condemn the attacks on Mozambique, on Zambia, on Angola, on Botswana, the threats against Lesotho, the destabilization efforts that are constantly being made in that area, the role played by the racist regimes of Rhodesia and South Africa. The pressing need for Zimbabwe and Namibia to be completely liberated quickly is not just a cause of the nonaligned countries or of the most progressive forces of our era, but is already contained in resolutions and agreements of the international community through the United Nations, and it implies duties that must be taken up and whose infractions must be denounced internationally.

Therefore, when in the final declaration the heads of state or government approved the condemnation by name of a number of Western countries, headed by the United States, for their direct or indirect collaboration in the maintenance of racist oppression and South Africa's criminal policy, and when on the other hand they recognized the role played by the nonaligned countries, the United Nations, the Organization of African Unity, the socialist countries, the Scandinavian countries, and other democratic and progressive forces in supporting the struggle of the peoples of Africa, this did not involve even the slightest manifestation of ideological leaning. It was simply the true expression of objective reality. To condemn South Africa without mentioning those who make its criminal policies possible would have been incomprehensible.

More forcibly and urgently than ever, the Sixth Summit Conference expressed the need not only to end the situation in which the Zimbabwean and Namibian peoples' right to independence is denied and the black men and women of South Africa's pressing need to attain a status in which they are considered as equal, respected human beings is denied, but also to guarantee conditions of respect and peace for all the countries of the region.

The continued support for the movements of national liberation, the Patriotic Front [of Zimbabwe] and SWAPO, was a decision that was as unanimous as it was expected. And let us state very clearly now that this is not a case of expressing a unilateral preference for solutions through armed struggle. It is true that the conference praised the people of Namibia, and of SWAPO which is their sole and authentic representative, for having stepped up the armed struggle and for advancing in it, and called for total and effective support for that form of combat. But that was due to the fact that the South African racists have slammed the door on any real negotiations and the fact that the efforts to achieve negotiated solutions go no farther than mere maneuvers.

The attitude toward the Commonwealth's decisions at its Lusaka meetings last August to have the British government, as an authority in Southern Rhodesia, call a conference to discuss the problems of Zimbabwe confirmed the fact that the nonaligned countries are not opposed to solutions that may be achieved without armed struggle, so long as they lead to the creation of an authentic majority government and so long as independence is achieved in a manner satisfactory to the fighting peoples, and that this be done in accordance with the resolutions of such bodies as the Organization of African Unity [OAU], the United Nations, and our own Nonaligned countries.

Mr President, the Sixth Summit once more had to express its regret over the fact that Resolution 1514 of the General Assembly of the United Nations, concerning the granting of independence to colonial countries and peoples, has not been applied to Western Sahara. We should recall that the decisions of the nonaligned countries and the resolutions of the United Nations, and more specifically General Assembly Resolution 3331, have all reaffirmed the inalienable rights of the people of Western Sahara to self-determination and independence.

In this problem Cuba feels a very special responsibility since it has been a member of the United Nations commission that investigated the situation in Western Sahara, and this enabled our representatives to verify the Saharawi people's total desire for self-determination and independence.

We repeat here that the position of the nonaligned countries is not one of antagonism against any country. The welcome that we gave to the agreement between the Republic of Mauritania and the Polisario Front and to the Republic of Mauritania's decision to withdraw its forces from the territory of Western Sahara is in keeping with the application of our principles and the agreements of the United Nations, as is our deploring the extension of Morocco's armed occupation of the southern part of Western Sahara, previously administered by Mauritania.

Therefore the conference expressed its hope that the ad-hoc committee established at the Sixteenth OAU Summit Conference would make it possible to insure that the people of the Sahara would be allowed to exercise their right to self-determination and independence as soon as possible.

That same principle and that same position determined the resolution on Mayotte and the Malagasy islands and the need for them to be reintegrated into the Comoros and Madagascar respectively.

Mr President, there can be no doubt that the problem of the Middle East has become one of the situations that give rise to the greatest concern in today's world. The Sixth Summit Conference examined it in its two-fold dimension.

On the one hand the conference reaffirmed that Israel's determination to continue to follow its policy of aggression, expansionism, and colonial settlement in the occupied territories, with the support of the United States, constitutes a serious threat to world peace and security.

The conference also examined the problem from the standpoint of the rights of the Arab countries and of the Palestinian question.

For the nonaligned countries the Palestinian question is the very crux of the problem of the Middle East. They both form an integral whole and neither can be settled in isolation from the other.

No just peace can be established in the region unless it is based on total and unconditional withdrawal by Israel from all the occupied Arab territories as well as the return to the Palestinian people of all their occupied territories and the restoration of their inalienable national rights, including their right to return to their homeland, to self-determination, and to the establishment of an independent state in Palestine in accordance with Resolution 3236 of the General Assembly.

This means that all measures taken by Israel in the occupied Palestinian and other Arab territories, including the establishment of colonies or settlements on Palestinian land or other Arab territories—whose immediate dismantlement is a prerequisite for a solution of the problem—are illegal, null, and void.

As I stated in my address to the Sixth Summit Conference, ". . . we are not fanatics. The revolutionary movement has always learned to hate racial discrimination and pogroms of any kind. From the bottom of our heart, we repudiate the merciless persecution and genocide that the Nazis once visited on the Jews, but there is nothing in recent history that parallels it more than the dispossession, persecution and genocide that imperialism and the Zionists are currently practicing against the Palestinian people.

"Pushed off their lands, expelled from their own country, scattered throughout the world, persecuted and murdered, the heroic Palestinians are a vivid example of sacrifice and patriotism, living symbols of the most terrible crime of our era."

Can anyone be surprised that the conference, for reasons that stemmed not from any political prejudice, but rather from an objective analysis of the facts, was obliged to point out that the United States' policy, in aligning itself with Israel and in supporting it and working to attain partial solutions that are favorable to Zionist aims and guarantee the fruits of Israel's aggression at the expense of the Palestinian Arab people and the entire Arab nation, played a major role in preventing the establishment of a just and comprehensive peace in the region?

The facts—and only the facts—led the conference to condemn the U.S. policies and maneuvers in that region.

When the heads of state or government arrived at the consensus that condemned the Camp David agreement and the Egyptian–Israeli treaty of March 1979, their formulations had been preceded by long hours of detailed study and fruitful exchanges which allowed the conference to consider those treaties not only as a complete abandonment of the cause of the Arab countries, but also as an act of complicity with the continuing occupation of Arab territories.

These words are harsh, but they are true and just. It is not the Egyptian people who have been subjected to the judgment of the Movement of Nonaligned Countries. The Egyptian people command the respect of each and every one of our countries, and enjoy the solidarity of all our peoples.

The same voices that were raised to denounce the Camp David

agreements and the Egyptian–Israeli treaty eulogized Gamal Abdel Nasser, a founder of the Movement and an upholder of the fighting traditions of the Arab nation. No one has been unaware and no one will ever be unaware of Egypt's historic role in Arab culture and development or of its merits as a founding nation and a driving force in the Movement of the Nonaligned Countries.

The conference also gave its attention to the problems of Southeast Asia. The growing conflicts and tensions that have been created in the region are a threat to peace that must be avoided.

Similar concern was expressed by the Sixth Summit Conference in relation to the situation of the Indian Ocean. The declaration adopted eight years ago by the United Nations General Assembly that the Indian Ocean should be a zone of peace has not been fulfilled. Far from being reduced the military presence in the region is growing. Military bases have now reached as far as South Africa, and are also serving as a means for surveillance against the African liberation movements. The talks between the United States and the Soviet Union are still suspended, despite the recent agreement between the two countries to discuss their resumption.

All this led to the Sixth Summit Conference's invitation to all states concerned to work effectively to fulfill the objectives of the declaration of the Indian Ocean as a zone of peace.

The Sixth Conference also analyzed other issues of regional and world interest, such as European security and cooperation, the problem of the Mediterranean, the tensions that still exist there and that have now been increased as a result of Israel's aggressive policy and the support given it by certain imperialist powers.

The conference also studied the situation in Cyprus, still partially occupied by foreign troops, and Korea, still divided despite the Korean people's desire for a unified homeland. This led the nonaligned states to reaffirm and broaden resolutions of solidarity aimed at fulfilling the aspirations of both peoples.

It would be impossible to refer to all the political decisions of the Sixth Summit Conference. If we were to do so we would be unable to touch upon what we consider to be one of the most fundamental aspects of that Sixth Summit Conference: namely its economic perspectives—the clamor of the people of the developing countries, weary as they are of their backwardness and the suffering it engenders. Cuba as the host country will present to all members of the international community copies of the conference's final declaration and additional resolutions. But before informing you of how the nonaligned countries view the world economic situation and what demands they make and what their hopes are, perhaps you will allow me to take a few more moments to inform you of the final declaration's approach concerning Latin American issues of the moment.

The fact that the Sixth Conference was held in Latin America gave the heads of state or government meeting there the opportunity to recall that the peoples of that region began their efforts to obtain independence at the very beginning of the nineteenth century. They also did not forget, as is said in the declaration, that "Latin America is one of the regions of the world that historically has suffered the most from the aggression of imperialism, colonialism and neo-colonialism from the United States and Europe."

The participants in the conference were forced to point out that remnants of colonialism, neocolonialism, and national oppression still remain in that area of struggle. Thus the conference spoke out in favor of the eradication of colonialism and all its forms and manifestations. It condemned the presence of foreign military bases in Latin America and the Caribbean, such as those in Cuba and Puerto Rico, and again demanded that the government of the United States and other colonial powers restore to those countries that part of their territory occupied by those bases against the will of their people.

The experience lived through in other areas led the heads of state or government to reject and condemn any attempt to create in the Caribbean a so-called "security force," a neocolonial mechanism which is incompatible with the sovereignty, peace, and security of these countries.

By calling for the restitution of the Malvinas Islands to the Republic of Argentina, by reaffirming its support for the inalienable right of the people of Belize to self-determination, independence, and territorial integrity, the conference once again gave evidence of what its declaration had defined as the very quintessence of nonalignment. It welcomed the fact that as of October 1 the treaties on the Panama Canal concluded between the Republic of Panama and the United States would enter into force. It gave its full support to those treaties and it called for their being fully respected in both letter and spirit, and called on all the states of the world to adhere to the protocol of the treaty concerning the permanent neutrality of the Panama Canal.

The heads of state and government reiterated their solidarity with the struggle of the Puerto Rican people and their inalienable right to self-determination, independence, and territorial integrity, despite all the pressure, the threats, and the flattery that was brought to bear by the U.S. government, and the demand that the issue of Puerto Rico be considered an internal question of the United States. And they called upon the government of the United States of America to refrain from any political or repressive maneuvers tending to perpetuate the colonial status of that country.

No more appropriate tribute could be paid to the Latin American traditions of freedom and to the heroic people of Puerto Rico, who in recent days have just celebrated another anniversary of the "Cry of Lares," which expressed their indomitable will for freedom almost one hundred years ago.

When speaking to the Latin American reality, the heads of state or government, who had already analyzed the significance of the liberating process that took place in Iran, could not fail to refer to the revolutionary upheaval in Grenada and the remarkable victory of the people of Nicaragua and their vanguard, the Sandinista National Liberation Front, and to emphasize the historic significance of that event for the peoples of Latin America and of the world. The heads of state or government also stressed something new in Latin American relations, something that sets an example for other regions of the world: namely the way in which the governments of Panama, Costa Rica, and Mexico, as well as the member countries of the subregional Andean Pact—Bolivia, Colombia, Ecuador, Peru, and Venezuela—acted in solidarity and unity to achieve a just solution of the Nicaraguan problem, as well as Cuba's traditional solidarity with that people's cause.

I confess that these considerations on Latin America would alone have justified the Cuban people's efforts and the work of the hundreds of thousands of men and women of our country who were determined to enable Cuba to give a worthy welcome to the fraternal nations of the Movement of Nonaligned Countries at the Havana Summit Conference. But for Cuba there was much more than this. There is something that, on behalf of our people, we would like to thank you for in this forum of the United Nations. In Havana, the Cuban people's right to choose their political and social system was supported, as was their claim to the territory occupied by the Guantánamo base, and the condemnation of the blockade with which the United States government continues its efforts to isolate the Cuban revolution, seeking to destroy it.

We appreciate the deep feeling and the universal resonance of the Movement's recent denunciation in Havana of the hostile acts, pressures, and threats against Cuba by the United States, declaring them to be a flagrant violation of the charter of the United Nations and of the principles of international law, as a threat to world peace.

Once again we respond to our brothers, assuring the international community that Cuba will remain true to the principles of international solidarity.

Mr President, history has taught us that when a people, freeing itself from a colonial or neocolonial system obtains its independence, it is at one and the same time the last act in a lengthy struggle and the first in a new and difficult battle. Because the independence, sovereignty, and freedom of our apparently free peoples are constantly threatened by foreign control over their natural resources, by financial impositions by official international bodies, and by the precarious situation of their economies, all of which reduce their full sovereignty.

For this reason, at the very beginning of their analysis of the world economic problems, the heads of state or government, "once again solemnly emphasized the paramount importance of consolidating political independence through economic emancipation . . . and they therefore reiterated that the existing international economic system runs counter to the basic interests of the developing countries and is profoundly unjust and incompatible with the development of the nonaligned countries and other developing countries, and does not contribute to the elimination of the economic and social evils that afflict those countries . . ."

And furthermore, they emphasized "the historic mission that the Movement of Nonaligned Countries should play in the struggle to obtain the economic and political independence of all developing countries and peoples; to exercise their full and permanent sovereignty and control over their natural and all other resources and economic activities; and to promote a fundamental restructuring of the world economy through the establishment of the new international economic order."

And the statement concludes with the following words: "The struggle to eliminate the injustice of the existing international economic system and to establish a new international economic order is an integral part of the people's struggle for political, economic, cultural, and social liberation."

It is not necessary to go into how profoundly unjust and incompatible with the development of the underdeveloped countries the existing international economic system is. The figures are already so well known that it unnecessary for us to repeat them here.

There are discussions on whether there are only 400 million undernourished people in the world or whether the figure has once again risen to 450 million, as certain international documents stated. Even 400 million hungry men and women constitute too heavy an accusation.

But nobody doubts that all the hopes that have been raised in the developing countries appear to have been dashed and extinguished at this ending of the second development decade.

The director-general of the Food and Agricultural Organization [FAO] council has acknowledged that "progress is still disappointingly slow in relation to the long-term development goals contained in the International Development Strategy, in the Declaration and Program of Action on the Establishment of the New International Economic Order, and in the Resolution of the World Food Conference and in several subsequent conferences." We are still far from having achieved the modest 4 percent annual average increase in the developing countries' food and agricultural production, which was proposed 10 years ago to solve some of the most pressing problems of world hunger and to approach consumption levels that are still low. As a result of this, food imports by the developing countries, which right now constitute an aggravating factor on their unfavorable balance of payments, will soon, according to FAO figures, reach unmanageable proportions.

In the face of this, official commitments of foreign aid to agriculture in the developing countries are falling off. This panorama cannot be prettied up. At times certain official documents reflect circumstantial increases in the agricultural production of some areas of the underdeveloped world, or stress the cyclical price increases registered by some agricultural items. But these are cases of transitory advances and of short-lived advantages.

The developing countries' agricultural export revenues are still unstable and insufficient to meet their import needs for food, fertilizers, and other items required to raise their own production. Per capita food production in Africa in 1977 was 11 percent below that of 10 years earlier.

While backwardness in agriculture is perpetuated, the process of industrialization cannot advance either. It cannot advance because most of the developed countries view the industrialization of the developing countries as a threat.

In 1975, the Lima World Conference on Industrialization proposed as a goal to the developing countries that we be responsible for 25 percent of the world's manufacturing output by the year

2000. But the progress made since that conference has been so insignificant that if the measures proposed by the Sixth Summit Conference are not implemented and if a crash program is not put into effect to modify the economic policies of most of the developed countries, that target will never be met. We now account for less than 9 percent of the world's manufactured output.

Our dependency is also expressed in the fact that the countries of Asia, Africa and Latin America import 26.1 percent of the manufactured goods that enter into international trade, and we export only 6.3 percent of them.

It may be said that some industrial expansion is taking place. But it does not take place at the necessary pace, nor in the key industries of industrial economy. This was pointed out at the Havana conference. The world redistribution of industry, the so-called industrial redeployment, should not consist of a new confirmation of the deep economic inequalities that emerged in the colonial era of the nineteenth century. At that time we were condemned to be producers of raw materials and cheap agricultural products. Now, an effort is being made to use the abundant labor power and starvation wages and to transfer to our countries the low technology industries, the industries of lowest productivity, and those that most pollute the environment. We categorically reject this.

The developed market-economy countries today absorb more than 85 percent of the world's manufactured goods, including those whose industrial production requires the highest technology. They also control more than 83 percent of all industrial exports and 26 percent of those exports go to the developing countries, whose markets they monopolize.

The most serious aspect of this dependent structure is that our imports—consumer items as well as capital goods—are all manufactured according to the demands, needs, and technology of the most developed industrial countries and the patterns of consumer societies, which are thus introduced through the chinks of our trade, contaminating our own societies, and in this way adding a new element to the already permanent structural crisis.

The result of all this, as was noted by the heads of state or government in Havana, is that the gap between the developed and developing countries not only persists, but has substantially increased. The relative share of the developing countries in the world output decreased considerably during the last two decades, which has still more disastrous effects on such problems as malnutrition, illiteracy, and poor sanitation.

Some would like to solve the tragic problem of humanity with drastic measures to reduce the population. They remember that wars and epidemics helped to reduce population in other eras. They wish to go even further. They want to blame underdevelopment on the population explosion.

But the population explosion is not the cause, but the result of underdevelopment. Development will bring solutions to the problems of poverty and also, through education and culture, will help our countries to attain rational and adequate rates of growth.

A recent report put out by the World Bank paints an even blacker picture. It is possible—the report says—that by the year 2000 some 600 million people on this earth may still be submerged in absolute poverty.

Mr President, distinguished representatives, the state of agricultural and industrial backwardness from which the developing countries have not managed to emerge is, as the Sixth Summit Conference pointed out, undoubtedly the result of unjust and unequal international relations. But, as the Havana declaration also points out, to this is now added the prolonged world economic crisis.

I shall not dwell too long on this aspect. Let us however state that we heads of state or government consider that the crisis of the international economic system is not a phenomenon of a cyclical nature, but is rather a symptom of the underlying structural maladjustments and of a disequilibrium that are part of its very nature; and that that imbalance has been aggravated by the refusal of the developed market-economy countries to control their external imbalances and their high rates of inflation and unemployment. That inflation has been engendered precisely in those developed countries that refuse now to implement the only measures that could eliminate it. And let us further point out, and this is something to which we will return later and which has also been set down in the Havana declaration, that this crisis is also the result of persisting inequality in international economic relations, so that eliminating the inequality, as we propose, will contribute to reducing and eliminating the crisis itself.

What are the main guidelines formulated in Havana by the representatives of the Movement of Nonaligned Countries?

We condemned the persistent diversion of human and material resources into an arms race which is unproductive, wasteful, and dangerous to humanity. And we demanded that a substantial part of the resources now devoted to arms, particularly by the major powers, be used for economic and social development.

We expressed our grave concern over the negligible progress that has been made in the negotiations for the implementation of the declaration and the program of action on the establishment of a new international economic order. We pointed out that this was due to the lack of political will on the part of most of the developed countries and we specifically censure the delaying, diversionary, and divisive tactics adopted by those countries. The failure of the fifth UNCTAD [UN Conference on Trade and Development] session highlighted that very situation.

We confirmed that the unequal exchange in international economic relations, defined as an essential characteristic of the system, has, if possible, become even more unequal. While the prices of manufactured goods, capital goods, foodstuffs, and services that we import from the developed countries are constantly rising, the prices of the raw materials we export are stagnating and are subject to constant fluctuation. The terms of exchange have worsened. We emphasized that protectionism, one of the factors aggravating the Great Depression of the 1930s, has been reintroduced by some developed countries.

The conference deplored the fact that in the GATT [General Agreement of Tariffs and Trade] negotiations the developed countries belonging to it did not take into account the interest and concerns of the developing countries, especially the least developed among them.

The conference also denounced the way in which certain developed countries are intensifying their use of domestic subsidies for certain products, to the detriment of the products of the developing nations.

The conference further deplored the shortcomings in the scope and operation of the Generalized System of Preferences, and in that spirit condemned the discriminatory restrictions contained in the United States Foreign Trade Act and the inflexible positions adopted by some developed countries, which prevented the adoption of an agreement on these problems at the fifth session of UNCTAD.

We expressed our concern over the constant deterioration of the international monetary situation. The instability of the exchange rate of the main reserve currencies, along with inflation, increases the imbalance in the world economic situation, creates additional economic difficulties for the developing countries, lowering the real value of their export earnings and reducing the value of their foreign currency reserves.

We also pointed out that the disorderly growth of international liquidity, mainly through the use of devalued United States dollars and other reserve currencies, is a negative factor. We noted that while the inequality of international economic relations is raising the developing countries' accumulated foreign debt to over $300 billion, the international financial bodies and the private banks are raising their interest rates, are imposing shorter terms of loan amortization, and are thus financially strangling the developing countries.

The conference denounced all this as constituting an element of coercion in negotiations, which allows them to obtain additional political and economic advantages at the expense of our countries.

The conference noted the neocolonialist determination to prevent the developing countries from exercising their full, effective, and permanent sovereignty over their natural resources and it reaffirmed this right. It was for this reason that it supported the efforts of raw-material producing developing countries to obtain just and remunerative prices for their exports and to improve, in real terms, their export earnings.

Moreover, the conference paid more attention than ever to the strengthening of economic relations and to scientific-technical and technological transfers among the developing countries. The concept of what could be defined as "collective self-reliance," that is, mutual support and collaboration among the developing countries, so that in the first place they will depend on their own collective forces, is given greater emphasis in the Havana declaration than ever before.

Cuba, as chair of the movement and coordinating country, intends together with the Group of 77 to do everything necessary to promote the program of action on economic cooperation drawn up by the conference.

Nevertheless, we cannot conceive of that "collective self reliance" as anything even remotely resembling self-sufficiency. Rather we consider it to be a factor in international relations that will mobilize all the possibilities and resources of that considerable and important part of humanity represented by the developing countries and incorporate them in the general current of resources and economies that can be mobilized in both the capitalist camp and the socialist countries.

Mr President, the Sixth Summit rejected the attempts of certain developed countries to try to use the question of energy to divide the developing nations.

The energy problem can only be examined in its historic context, by taking into account the fact that the wasteful consumption patterns of some of the developed countries and the role played by transnational oil corporations has led to the squandering of hydrocarbons, and by noting the plundering role of transnational corporations, which have benefited from cheap energy supplies—which they have used irresponsibly—up until only recently. The transnationals have been exploiting both the producers and consumers and reaping unjustified windfall profits, while at the same time falsifying facts by shifting the blame for the present situation onto the developing countries that are exporters of oil.

Permit me to recall that in my opening remarks to the conference I pointed out the desperate situation of the non-oil-producing underdeveloped countries, especially the least developed ones, and I expressed my confidence that the nonaligned oil-producing countries would devise formulas to help alleviate the unfavorable situation of those countries that had already been hit by the world inflation and unequal trade relations, and who suffer serious balance-of-payments deficits and sharp increases in their foreign debts. But this does not obviate the principal responsibility of the developed countries, their monopolies, and their transnational corporations.

The heads of state or government, adopting this approach to the energy issue, stressed that this subject should be the main focus of global negotiations within the United Nations, with the participation of all countries and linking the energy question to all the development problems, to financial and monetary reforms, to world trade and raw materials, so as to make a comprehensive and global analysis of the aspects which have a bearing on the establishment of the new international economic order.

No review of the main problems confronting the developing countries within the context of the world economy would be complete without an examination of the functioning of the transnational corporations. Once again their policies and practices were declared unacceptable. It was charged that in their search for profits they exhaust the resources, distort the economy, and violate the sovereignty of developing countries. They undermine the rights of people to self-determination. They violate the principles of noninterference in the affairs of states. And they frequently resort to bribery, corruption, and other undesirable practices, through which they seek to subordinate—and succeed in subordinating the developing countries to the industrialized countries.

In view of the inadequate progress achieved in the work carried out within the United Nations for drawing up a code of conduct to regulate the activities of transnational corporations, the conference reaffirmed the urgency of early completion of this work, in order to provide the international community with a legal instrument with which at least to control and regulate the activities of the transnational corporations in accordance with the objectives and aspirations of the developing countries.

In setting forth all the overwhelming negative aspects in the economic situation of developing countries, the Sixth Summit called special attention to the mounting problems of the least developed, the most disadvantaged, the landlocked countries, and those isolated in the hinterlands, and asked that urgent measures be adopted to alleviate their problems.

That, Mr President, distinguished representatives, was the far from optimistic, rather somber, and discouraging picture which the members of the Nonaligned Movement had in mind when they met in Havana. But the nonaligned countries did not allow themselves to be swept into positions of frustration or exasperation, however understandable that might have been. While drawing up strategic concepts for advancing and continuing in their struggle, the heads of state or government repeated their demands and defined their positions.

The first and fundamental objective in our struggle consists of reducing and finally eliminating the unequal exchange that prevails today and converts international trade into a very useful vehicle for the plundering of our wealth. Today the product of one hour's labor in the developed countries is exchanged for ten hours of labor in the underdeveloped countries.

The nonaligned countries demand that serious attention be paid to the integrated program for commodities, which up until now has been manipulated and juggled in the so-called North-South negotiations. In the same way, we demand that the Common Fund, which was projected as an instrument of stabilization that would establish a permanent linkage between the prices we receive for our products and those paid for our imports, and which has scarcely begun to have impact, be given a big boost.

For the nonaligned countries this linkage—which permanently ties the prices of their export items with the prices of basic equipment, industrial products, raw materials, and technology that they import from the developed countries—constitutes an essential pivot for all future economic negotiations.

The developing countries demand that the countries that have created inflation and have stimulated it through their policies adopt the necessary measures to control it and thus put an end to the aggravation of the unequal exchange between our countries.

The developing countries demand—and will continue their struggle to achieve—access to the markets of the developed countries for the industrial products of their incipient economies; a halt to the vicious protectionism that has been reintroduced in the international economy and that threatens once again to lead us into a murderous economic war; and that nonreciprocal tariff preferences be applied generally and without deceptive falsehoods so that the young industries of the developing countries can be developed without being crushed in the world market by the superior technological resources of the developed countries.

The nonaligned countries consider that the negotiations which are about to be concluded on the law of the sea should not be used as certain developed countries seek to use them—to ratify and endorse the exisiting imbalance as regards sea resources—but should serve as a vehicle for equitable redress. The conference on the law of the sea has once again brought out and stressed the arrogance and imperialist determination of some countries which, placing their technological possibilities ahead of the spirit of understanding and accommodation requested by the developing nations, threaten to take unilateral action in carrying out deep-sea mining operations.

The foreign debt of the developing countries has now risen to $335 billion. It is estimated that about $40 billion a year goes to servicing this foreign debt, which represents more than 20 percent of their exports. Moreover, the average per capita income in the developed countries is now 14 times that of the underdeveloped countries. This situation is insupportable.

The developing countries need the establishment of a new system of financing, enabling them to obtain the necessary financial resources to ensure continuous and independent development of their economies. These financing methods should be long-term and low-interest. The use of these financial resources should be completely at the disposition of the developing countries. This will enable them to establish a system of priorities for their own economies, in accordance with their own plans for industrial development, and it will help prevent those funds from being absorbed, as they are today, by transnational corporations, which use alleged financial contributions for development to aggravate the distortions of the developing countries' economies and reap maximum profits from the exploitation of these countries' resources.

The developing countries, and on their behalf the Movement of Nonaligned Countries, demand that a substantial portion of the immense resources now being squandered by humanity on the arms race be dedicated to development, which would both contribute to reducing the danger of war and to helping improve the international situation.

Expressing the position of all the developing countries, the nonaligned countries call for the establishment of a new international monetary system, which will put an end to the disastrous fluctuations to which the main currencies used in the international economy, especially the United States dollar, are subject. The financial disorder also hits the developing countries, which hope that when the outlines of the new international monetary system are drawn up, they, as the majority of the countries in the international community, representing as they do more than 1.5 billion men and women, may be given a voice in the decision-making process.

Summing up, Mr President, distinguished representatives:

Unequal exchange is ruining our peoples. It must end!

Inflation, which is being exported to us, is crushing our peoples. It must end!

Protectionism is impoverishing our people. It must end!

The existing imbalance in the exploitation of the resources of the sea is abusive. It must be abolished!

The financial resources received by the developing countries are insufficient. They must be increased!

Arms expenditures are irrational. They must cease and the funds thus released must be used to finance development!

The international monetary system prevailing today is bankrupt. It must be replaced!

The debts of the least developed countries, and of those in a disadvantageous position, are burdens impossible to bear, and have no solution. They must be cancelled!

Indebtedness oppresses the rest of the developing countries economically. There must be relief!

The economic chasm between the developed countries and the

countries seeking development, is not narrowing but widening. It must be closed!

These are demands of the underdeveloped countries.

Mr President, distinguished representatives:

Response to these demands, some of which have been systematically presented by the developing countries in international forums through the Group of 77 and by the Movement of Non-aligned Countries, would permit a change of course in the international economic situation that would provide the developing countries with the institutional conditions for organizing programs that would definitely place them on the road to development.

But even if all these measures were implemented, even if all the mistakes and evils of the present system of international relations were rectified, the developing countries would still lack one decisive element: international financing.

All the domestic and internal efforts, all the sacrifices that the peoples of the developing countries are making and are willing to make, and all the opportunities for increasing the economic potential that could be achieved by eliminating the inequality between the prices of their exports and those of imports and by improving the conditions in which their foreign trade is carried out, would not be enough.

In the light of their true financial situation at present, they need further resources to be able both to pay their debts and to make the enormous expenditures required on a global level for the jump into development. Here again, the figures are far too well known to require repeating.

The Sixth Summit Conference was concerned not only because the debts of the underdeveloped countries were practically unbearable, but also because that debt was growing yearly at an alarming rate. The data contained in the recent World Bank report, which came out while we were holding the conference in Havana, confirmed that the situation was growing worse daily. In 1978 alone, the foreign public debt of ninety-six developing countries rose by $51 billion. This rate of growth has raised the foreign debt to the astronomical figures already mentioned.

We cannot, Mr President, resign ourselves to this gloomy prospect!

The most renowned economists, both Western and those who ascribe to Marxist concepts, admit that the system of international indebtedness of the developing countries is completely irrational and that its persistence could lead to a sudden interruption that might endanger the entire precarious and unstable balance of the world economy.

Some try to explain the surprising economic fact that the international banking centers continue to provide funds to countries that are technically bankrupt by arguing that these are generous contributions to help those countries meet their economic difficulties. But this is not so. In fact, it is an operation for saving the international capitalist order itself. In October 1978, the Commission of European Communities admitted by way of clarification:

"The present balance of the world economy depends to a considerable extent on continuing the flow of private loans to non-oil-producing developing countries . . . on a scale unprecedented prior to 1974, and any obstacle to that flow will endanger that balance."

World financial bankruptcy would be very hard, most of all for the underdeveloped countries and the workers in the developed capitalist countries. It would also affect even the most stable socialist economies. But it is doubtful that the capitalist system would be able to survive such a catastrophe. And it would be difficult for the resulting dreadful economic situation not to inevitably engender a world conflagration. There is already talk of special military forces to occupy the oil fields and the sources of other raw materials.

But if it is the duty of everyone to be concerned over this somber prospect, it is first of all the duty of those who possess the greatest wealth and material abundance.

In any case, the prospect of a world without capitalism is not too frightening to us revolutionaries.

It has been proposed that instead of a spirit of confrontation we employ a sense of world economic interdependency that will enable us to call on the resources of all our economies to obtain joint benefits. But the concept of interdependency is acceptable only when you start by admitting the intrinsic and brutal injustice of the present interdependency.

The developing countries will not accept the unjust, arbitrary international division of labor which modern colonialism imposed on them with the English industrial revolution and which was widened and deepened by imperialism as "interdependency."

If we wish to avoid confrontation and struggle, which seem to be the only road open to the developing countries—a road that offers

long and arduous battles whose proportions no one can predict—
then we must all seek and find formulas for cooperation to solve
the great problems, which, while affecting our peoples, cannot be
solved without also affecting the most developed countries in one
way or another.

Not so many years ago we stated that the irrational squandering
of material goods and the subsequent waste of economic resources
by developed capitalist society had already become intolerable. Is
that not the cause of the dramatic energy crisis that we face right
now? Who, if not the non-oil-producing underdeveloped countries,
are bearing the main brunt of it?

This sentiment of the necessity of putting an end to the waste of
resources by the consumer societies is very widely held. A recent
document of the United Nations Industrial Development Organization states, "The present way of life, especially in the industrialized
countries, may have to undergo a radical and painful change."

Naturally, the developing countries cannot and do not hope that
the transformation they seek and the financing they require will
come to them as a gift following mere analyses on international
economic problems. In this process, which implies contradictions,
struggles, and negotiations, the nonaligned countries must first of
all depend upon their own decisions and efforts.

That conviction emerges clearly from the Sixth Summit Conference. In the economic portion of the final declaration, the heads of
state or government acknowledge the need to carry out in their
countries the necessary economic and social structural changes,
considering that this is the only way to eliminate the present
vulnerability of their economies and to turn a simple statistical
growth into genuine development.

The heads of state and government recognize that only thus will
their people be willing to pay the price required of them to become
the main protagonists in the process. As I said on that occasion, "If
the system is socially just, the possibilities of survival and economic and social development are incomparably greater."

The history of my own country provides irrefutable proof of this.

The emerging and crying need to solve the problem of underdevelopment brings us back, Mr President, to the problem I
mentioned a little while ago, and which is the last one I should like
to submit to this 34th Session of the General Assembly. I refer
specifically to international financing.

One of the most serious phenomena that accompany the accelerated indebtedness of the developing countries, as we have already

said, consists of the fact that the majority of the funds they receive from outside have to cover their trade balances and negative current accounts, renew their debts, and make interest payments.

If we take as an example the non-oil-exporting developing countries to whose situation I referred at the Havana conference, we note that in the last six years alone they have run up deficits in their balance of payments of over $200 billion.

In view of this, the investments required by the developing countries are enormous and they need them primarily, and with practically no exception, in those branches of production that yield low profits and therefore do not appeal to private foreign lenders or investors.

To increase the production of foodstuffs so as to do away with the malnutrition that afflicts those 450 million persons I mentioned earlier, we must provide many new land and water resources. According to specialized estimates, 76 million more hectares of land in the developing countries would have to be cultivated, and over 10 million more hectares of land irrigated in the next ten years to meet these needs.

Irrigation systems for 45 million hectares of land would have to be repaired. And therefore, even the most modest estimates admit—and I refer to aid and not the total flow of resources—that between $8 billion and $9 billion a year will be required to obtain an agricultural growth rate of from 3.5 to 4 percent in the developing countries.

With regard to industrialization, the estimates are far higher. The United Nations Conference on Industrial Development, when defining the goals for the Lima session, stated that at the heart of international development policy there should stand a target to be achieved in the year 2000 of annual levels of between $450 billion and $500 billion a year, of which a third, that is, from $150 billion to $160 billion, will have to be financed from external sources.

But Mr President, distinguished representatives, development includes more than agriculture and industrialization. Development primarily involves attention to human beings, who should be the protagonists and goal of all development efforts.

To cite the example of Cuba alone, I will point out that during the last five years our country has invested an average of nearly $200 million a year in school construction. Investment in medical equipment and construction of public health facilities averages over $40 million a year. And Cuba is only one of nearly 100 developing countries, and one of the smallest in terms of geography and population.

Therefore, it can be deduced that the developing countries will need billions of dollars more invested every year to overcome the results of backwardness in education and in public health services.

This is the big problem that faces us.

And that is not, gentlemen, our problem alone, a problem solely for the countries victimized by underdevelopment and insufficient development. It is a problem for the international community as a whole.

On more than one occasion it has been said that we were forced into underdevelopment by colonization and imperialist neocolonization. Therefore the task of helping us to emerge from underdevelopment is first and foremost a historic and moral obligation for those who benefited from the plunder of our wealth and the exploitation of our men and women for decades and for centuries.

But it is at the same time the task of humanity as a whole, as was stated at the Sixth Summit Conference.

The socialist countries did not participate in the plunder of the world and they are not responsible for the phenomena of underdevelopment. But even so, because of the nature of their social system, in which international solidarity is a premise, they understand and assume the obligation of helping to overcome it.

Likewise, when the world expects the oil-producing developing countries to contribute to the universal flow of external financing for development, it does not do so as a function of historic obligations and duties that no one can impose, but because of a hope for and a duty of solidarity among underdeveloped countries. The big oil exporting countries should be aware of their responsibilities.

Even those developing countries that are relatively more advanced should make their contributions. Cuba, which is not speaking here on behalf of its own interests and which is not defending here a national objective, is willing to contribute, in accordance with its means, thousands or tens of thousands of technicians: doctors, teachers, agronomists, hydraulic engineers, mechanical engineers, economists, middle-level technicians, skilled workers, and so on.

The time has therefore come for all of us to join in the task of drawing entire peoples, hundreds of millions of human beings, out of the backwardness, poverty, malnutrition, disease, and illiteracy that keep them from enjoying full human dignity and pride.

We therefore must mobilize our resources for development, and this is our joint obligation.

Mr President, there are so many special multilateral funds, both public and private, whose purpose is to contribute to some aspect of development, be it agricultural or industrial, or meeting deficits in the balance of payments. Therefore it is not easy for me, on presenting to this 34th Session of the General Assembly a report on the economic problems discussed at the Sixth Summit Conference of Nonaligned Countries, to formulate a concrete proposal for the establishment of a new fund.

But there can be no doubt that the problem of financing should be discussed thoroughly and fully in order to find a solution to it. In addition to the resources already mobilized by various banking channels, loan organizations, international bodies, and private finance agencies, we must discuss and decide upon the strategy for the next development decade, so that in that strategy we will include an additional contribution of not less than $300 billion at 1977 real value, to be invested in the underdeveloped countries and to be made in yearly installments of at least $25 billion from the very beginning. This aid should be in the form of donations and long-term moderate- and low-interest credits.

It is imperative that these additional funds be mobilized as the contribution of the developed world and of other countries with resources to the underdeveloped world over the next 10 years.

If we want peace, these resources will be required. If there are no resources for development there will be no peace. Some may think that we are asking too much, but I think that the figure itself is still modest. According to statistical information, as I stated in the inaugural session of the Sixth Summit Conference of Non-aligned Countries, the world military expenditures amount to more than $300 billion.

With $300 billion you could in one year build 600,000 schools with a capacity for 400 million children; 60 million comfortable homes for 300 million people; 30,000 hospitals with 18 million beds; 20,000 factories with jobs for more than 20 million workers; or you could build irrigation systems to water 150 million hectares of land, which with appropriate technology could feed a billion people. Humanity wastes this much every year on its military spending.

Moreover, consider further the enormous waste of youthful human resources, of technicians, of scientists, of fuel, raw materials, and other items. This is the fabulous price of preventing a true climate of confidence and peace from existing in the world.

The United States alone will in the 1980s spend six times this much on military activities.

We are requesting less for 10 years of development than is spent in a single year by the ministries of war, and much less than a tenth of what will be spent for military purposes in 10 years.

Some may consider our demand irrational. But where the true irrationality lies is in the world's madness in our era and the peril that threatens humanity. The enormous responsibility of studying, organizing, and distributing these amounts of resources should be entrusted entirely to the United Nations. These funds should be administered by the international community itself on an absolutely equal basis for all countries, whether they be contributors or beneficiaries, without any political conditions, and without the amount of the donations having anything to do with the voting power and deciding when loans are to be granted and to whom.

Even though the flow of resources should be measured in financial terms, it should not consist only of money. It may well be made up of equipment, fertilizer, raw materials, fuel, and complete factories valued in the terms of international trade. Aid in the form of technical personnel and their training should also be considered as a contribution.

We are convinced, Mr President, distinguished representatives, that if the secretary general of the United Nations, with the assistance of the president of the General Assembly, with all the prestige and weight of this organization behind them, and further supported from the very outset by the backing that the developing countries and especially the Group of 77 could and would give that initiative—we are convinced that we would be able to call together the various factors we have mentioned and initiate discussions in which there would be no room for the so-called North-South, East-West antagonisms, joining together instead all forces in a common undertaking, a common duty, a common hope. And that is how this idea that we are now submitting to the General Assembly could be crowned with success.

This is not a project that will benefit only the developing nations. It will benefit all countries.

As revolutionaries we are not afraid of confrontation. We have placed our trust in history and peoples. But as spokesperson and interpreter of the feelings of 95 nations, I have the duty to struggle to achieve cooperation among people, a cooperation which if obtained on a new and just basis will benefit all countries comprising the international community and will especially improve the prospects for peace.

Development in the short-term view may well be a task entailing apparent sacrifices and even donations which may seem irrecoverable. But the vast world now living submerged in backwardness with no purchasing power and extremely limited consumer capacity will, with its development, add a flood of hundreds of millions of consumers and producers to the international economy. It is only in this way that the international economy can be rehabilitated and help the developing countries emerge from the crisis in which they are submerged.

The history of international trade has shown that development is the most dynamic factor. A major portion of the trade of today takes place among fully industrialized countries. We can assure you that as industrialization and progress spread throughout the world, so trade will also spread to the benefit of all.

And it is for this reason that on behalf of the developing countries we advocate our cause and we ask you to support it. But this is not a gift which we seek. If we do not come up with effective solutions we will all be equal victims of the catastrophe.

Mr President, distinguished representatives, human rights are very often spoken of, but we must also speak of humanity's rights.

Why should some people go barefoot, so that others may ride in expensive cars?

Why should some live only thirty-five years, so that others may live seventy?

Why should some be miserably poor, so that others be exaggeratedly rich?

I speak on behalf of the children of the world who don't even have a piece of bread. I speak on behalf of the sick who lack medicine. I speak on behalf of those who have been denied the right to life and to human dignity.

Some countries are on the sea, others are not. Some have energy resources, others do not. Some possess abundant land on which to produce food, others do not. Some are so glutted with machinery and factories that even the air cannot be breathed because of the poisoned atmosphere. And others have only their own emaciated arms with which to earn their daily bread.

In short, some countries possess abundant resources, other have nothing. What is their fate? To starve? To be eternally poor? Why then civilization? Why then the conscience of man? Why then the United Nations? Why then the world?

You cannot speak of peace on behalf of tens of millions of human beings all over the world who are starving to death or dying of curable diseases. You cannot speak of peace on behalf of 900 million illiterates.

The exploitation of the poor countries by the rich must cease.

I know that there are exploiters and those who are exploited in many poor countries as well.

I address myself to the rich nations, asking them to contribute. And I address myself to the poor nations, asking them to distribute.

Enough of words! We need deeds!

Enough of abstractions. We want concrete action! Enough of speaking about a speculative new international order, which nobody understands. We must now speak of a real, objective order which everybody understands!

I have not come here as a prophet of the revolution. I have not come here to ask or to wish that the world be violently convulsed. I have come to speak of peace and cooperation among the peoples. And I have come to warn that if we do not peacefully and wisely solve and eliminate the present injustices and inequalities, the future will be apocalyptic.

The noise of weapons, of threatening language, and of overbearing behavior on the international arena must cease.

Enough of the illusion that the problems of the world can be solved by nuclear weapons. Bombs may kill the hungry, the sick, and the ignorant but bombs cannot kill hunger, disease, and ignorance. Nor can bombs kill the righteous rebellion of the peoples. And in the holocaust, the rich, who are the ones with the most to lose in this world, will also die.

Let us say farewell to arms, and let us in a civilized manner dedicate ourselves to the most pressing problems of our times. This is the responsibility, this is the most sacred duty of the statesmen of all the world. Moreover, this is the basic premise for human survival.

I thank you.

'Pushed off their lands, expelled from their country, scattered throughout the world, persecuted and murdered, the heroic Palestinians are a vivid example of sacrifice and patriotism, living symbols of the most terrible crime of our era.'

There is no peace without development

The Ministerial Meeting in New Delhi is a fitting setting to celebrate the historical date when, 20 years ago, on September 1961, the heads of state of government from 25 countries met in Belgrade to found the Movement of Nonaligned Countries and lay the foundations of that force entering the international arena.

On this memorable occasion, our first thoughts should be for those who had faith in the new idea and showed the creative determination to implement it. The figures of Nehru, Tito and Nasser, who are no longer with us, rise up as symbols of that group of statesmen.

The thrust that led to setting up the Movement, whose singular nature has become increasingly evident over the last two decades, emerged from the context of the crisis of the colonial and neocolonial system and as one of its most important consequences. In their historic first Declaration, the heads of state of government noted that the situation, which threatened at the time to lead to a world conflict, was the result of "the transition from an old order based on domination to a new order based on cooperation between nations." In reviewing contemporary problems, they observed that "the dynamic process and forms of social change often result in, or represent, a conflict between the old established order and the

---

The following message was sent to a ministerial meeting of the Movement of Nonaligned Countries in New Delhi, India, on the occasion of the 20th anniversary of the founding of the Movement. The message by Fidel Castro was sent as chair of the Movement.

new emerging nationalist forces." From that analysis, they reached a common conclusion which is an essential tenet of our actions:

"A lasting peace can be achieved only if this confrontation leads to a world where the domination of colonialism, imperialism and neocolonialism in all their manifestations are radically eliminated."

When meeting in 1961, the founders of the Movement of Nonaligned Countries recognized the problems resulting from the emergence to independence of a steadily growing number of countries that were breaking loose from the old colonial empire. They also saw the circumstances endangering world peace at the time. The cold war was threatening to give way to an actual war. Tension was mounting to a dangerous level.

It was to the credit of the founders of our Movement and proof of their great political foresight to have linked the struggle for universal just peace the peoples were striving for to the struggle to eliminate the old order based on domination and oppression that stubbornly persisted and was threatening peace. There is still validity to the tenet that true peace can only be attained in a world where domination by colonialism, imperialism and neocolonialism in all their manifestations are radically eliminated.

The Movement of Nonaligned Countries expressed its unshakable faith in the international community's ability to survive without having to resort to war as an instrument to solve differences. It followed the premise that the contradictions between opposite social systems—a sign of the times—were not an unsurmountable obstacle for peace, provided that attempts at dominating peoples and interfering with their development were eliminated once and for all.

Although the emerging force only comprised 25 countries at the time, the founders of the Movement understood that the fact that they gathered at the first conference was in itself an expression of a broader and deeper trend that could contribute to the definite improvement of the international situation. The Declaration stated: "Imperialism is weakening. Colonial empires and other forms of foreign oppression of peoples in Asia, Africa and Latin America are gradually disappearing and becoming a thing of the past." That is why the member countries, fully confident of the potential of the instrument they were creating, expressed their conviction that "the existence and the activities of the nonaligned countries in the interests of peace are one of the most important factors for safeguarding world peace."

To understand the undeniable validity of the historical view shown by the 25 founding countries in believing in the powerful, future development of the Movement of Nonaligned Countries, let us recall that when the first Declaration was signed, Algeria had yet to consolidate its independence. The Movement's documents denounced the "intolerable measures of repression taken by the Portuguese colonial authorities against the people of Angola" and demanded "the immediate evacuation of French armed forces from the whole of Tunisia." Colonialism obstinately sought to preserve its hold over Africa by turning its overt colonialism into subtle neocolonialism. Likewise, it refused to be displaced from Asia, thus heralding the unforgettable ordeal the heroic people of Vietnam were to be subjected to years later.

It soon became evident, however, that the founders of the Movement of Nonaligned Countries were not mistaken when they felt that they had started a force that was to grow and become an important factor in world politics.

Three years later, in Cairo, 45 member countries and 11 observers met, thereby attesting to the Movement's vigorous development. What's more, as stated in the Cairo Declaration, the peoples still under colonial domination and those "whose rights and sovereignty were being violated by imperialism and neocolonialism," showed a growing interest in the role of the Movement.

The Sixth Summit Conference in Havana corroborated the fact that 20 years after its foundation, the Movement of Nonaligned Countries is one of the major forces in contemporary life, a factor that cannot be overlooked in attempts to resolve the problems of our times. And this is true despite the vicissitudes of the complex international situation and the efforts made from both outside and inside the Movement to alter its character or dismember it, taking advantage of its inevitable heterogeneity. The presence in Havana of 94 member countries, national liberation movements and organizations, and 19 observers, and the fact that the Havana meeting was attended by a larger number of heads of state or government than had ever assembled in the history of international relations, are an indication that the Nonaligned Movement represents the clear majority of the international community and expresses the militant political positions of the underdeveloped and developing countries.

The undeniable influence of the Nonaligned Movement on international developments and its ability to speak on behalf of a majority of the world's states, which at the same time are free to express their own independent opinions, grants it unquestionable authority and responsibilities that cannot be evaded. On this 20th anniversary, therefore, its urgent message should reach all corners of the earth.

The Sixth Summit Conference, inspired by the optimism that has characterized the Movement since the beginning, reflected all the promising possibilities presented by the international situation. Above all, it had confidence in the peoples' aspiration for peace and their determination to attain it. But when we met in Havana, in September 1979, we noted in forceful and urgent terms the worrisome step backwards away from international détente, the visible dangers threatening peace and the direct and indirect effects of this process on our peoples.

Although the factors and forces sustaining our optimism regarding the future of humanity are still present and acting, unfortunately, the latest developments and the tendencies are not cause for optimism.

The steps away from détente run the risk of becoming permanent. Worse still, there are those who advocate replacing détente by a new cold war. SALT II, which was drawn up through meticulous and difficult bilateral negotiations, was discarded unilaterally. The concept of a balance between the great powers that could lead to progressive disarmament and denuclearization is being rejected and instead the search for "military superiority" has been proclaimed. This can only intensify the arms race and lead to increasing the nuclear threat or to nuclear war itself.

Based on that premise, where blackmail replaces good faith, global strategies emerge which have negative repercussions for all peoples.

The events in Afghanistan, in Iran and the war between this country and Iraq have served as a pretext to send to the Indian Ocean the largest number of warships ever seen before in that region, to further build up the Diego Garcia base and seek new bases in the Middle East and the Red Sea, thus undermining the intentions of the countries in the area—supported by the Non-aligned Movement—of turning the Indian Ocean into a zone of peace.

This worldwide situation, in which the most aggressive imperialist forces come to the fore, encourages the specific designs of the enemies of the peoples. The failure of the Geneva Conference on Namibia shows us that the South African racists—whose ignominious system of apartheid has been condemned by the Movement of

Nonaligned Countries since its first Declaration in 1961—are now confident that the emerging cold war atmosphere will enable them to continue their racial violence against black citizens and prolong their illegal domination of Namibia. This explains their cynical, brutal attack against Mozambique. Likewise, the new imperialist military bases in the Horn of Africa encourage vengeful and expansionist designs on revolutionary Ethiopia. The Israeli Zionists feel equally encouraged and shamelessly attack Lebanon. The military tyrannies in Latin America and the Caribbean are expecting and, in some cases, are already receiving greater support from abroad to use against their peoples. Open threats are being made in this region to intervene in Central America and the Caribbean, especially against the heroic people of El Salvador, as a means to block the independence and democratic change aspired to by the overwhelming majority. Cuba faces the great declared danger of total blockade, as well as threats of direct military aggression. In Europe, the scene of the most intense efforts by the forces that have fought for peace and détente, attempts are being made to renew the arms race and break the delicate nuclear equilibrium. Today peace is once again the center of our attention.

It would be difficult to decide whether the danger of war was greater in 1961, when the heads of state or government made the first dramatic appeal, than it is now, 20 years later. The history of these two decades shows the extent to which the nonaligned countries, together with all peace-loving forces in the various geographic areas and social spheres, have contributed to having détente prevail, the strengthening of the idea that peace is more than a truce between great powers, and the conviction that there will be peace only when the proper conditions are guaranteed and when its benefits encompass all countries regardless of their size and geographic location.

Hence, on this 20th anniversary, the permanent search for peace, understood in its universal dimension, is, as it was in 1961, the first and most important obligation of our Movement. The appeal we then addressed to those powers which had the dramatic possibility of unleashing a new war, urging them to embark upon the path of negotiations, has bitter validity. But this is not enough. Peace is not, and cannot be the exclusive responsibility of those who have material resources with which to start a global war. We, the countries not committed to a military alliance, have something to say and a task ahead of us. The Movement's firm presence in the search for conditions of peace, together with the working class, the intellectuals in developed industrialized countries and the states that have placed peace at the heart of their international politics, form a decisive joint force to impede the sinister prospect of a nuclear holocaust.

The nonaligned countries should, therefore, make an urgent attempt to implement the decisions of the Sixth Summit Conference on this problem, considering that the changes that have taken place in the international arena make the situation even more disturbing and the activity of the Movement even more pressing.

The great problem of peace is indissolubly linked to the other major preoccupation which has been at the center of the Movement's activities during these 20 years: development.

We have said: "There can be no peace without development." Allow us to repeat it.

In 1961, the Movement set forth the undeferable objective of ending all types of neocolonialism and imperialist domination. To this purpose it demanded first of all the elimination of all interference or intervention in other countries, so that they could peacefully and freely exercise their rights to full independence, as well as respect for their territorial integrity. From those early days the right of every country to freely control and use their natural resources was established.

But the founding conference went even further. Considering the disparity and the lack of economic equality which the developing countries inherited from colonialism and imperialism, it demanded that efforts be exerted to eliminate them. To this aim it prepared an initial program that was developed in Cairo, Lusaka, the ministerial meeting in Georgetown and Algiers and was confirmed by the Colombo and Havana summit conferences, and enriched by the debates at the United Nations and the other international forums held in past years.

But it is important to recognize that, far from improving, the situation of the developing countries—particularly the non-oil-producing and, especially the group suffering from disadvantageous conditions—has become even more unbearable.

The subsequent conferences of Nonaligned Countries and the declarations of the Group of 77 openly pointed out the responsibility the more developed capitalist countries have for that stagnation of negotiations, whose lack of political will to advance towards mutually advantageous solutions has become evident. Unequal exchange in international trade, monopoly over technology, manipulation of the crisis-riddled monetary system and the shortage of financing are permanent elements of a frustrated dialogue in which the developing countries have yet to be listened to.

In 1973, our unforgettable chairman, Houari Boumedienne, submitted to the United Nations the economic program the Nonaligned Countries proposed to first mitigate and later permanently close the growing gap between the living standards of our countries and those of the developed countries which the Belgrade conference had emphasized.

That program was not given adequate attention.

As of 1974, the continuous and intermittent crisis of the capitalist system, the development of inflation provoked mainly by the artificial financing of the war against Vietnam, and the emergence of the energy problem as one of the challenges facing humanity all coincided. Thus, the situation of the developing countries has become even more desperate.

Neocolonialism, repudiated in 1961, has penetrated into most of the countries that attained their precarious independence in the past 20 years, under surreptitious control by the multinational enterprises.

In the 34th United Nations General Assembly, speaking on behalf of the Nonaligned Movement to present the results of the Sixth Summit Conference and renew our proposals, I denounced this overwhelming and growing inequality in the manner decided by the conference. In reviewing the risks of the financial bankruptcy threatening the developing countries whose foreign debt is $400 billion with annual deficits in the balance of payment of some $70 billion, I proposed that the international community—in particular, the developed countries and along with them the oil-supplying developing countries—guarantee a flow of resources to the developing countries in the present decade, in addition to the notoriously insufficient resources they are already receiving. At the time, I set a target for the decade of no less than $300 billion in 1977 real terms. Other recent studies have mentioned even higher figures. The General Assembly decided that this proposal should be discussed by the organizations entrusted with the preparation of global negotiations, but we must confess that once again there has been a lack of receptivity by those that should respond.

Under these circumstances, the new international economic order and the charter of economic rights and duties of states—which the Movement supported vigorously from the start—continue to be distant hopes which are constantly frustrated.

We are convinced that the economic proposals we, the developing countries, have submitted for discussion represent a rational solution to the problems of our time that will not only contribute to the elimination of obstacles and stimulate the economies of our countries but will revitalize the entire international economy for the benefit of each one of its sectors. The Movement of Non-aligned Countries will continue to pay special attention to this situation and should be present at every international event aimed at discussing these problems and finding adequate solutions.

Therefore, we must continue to consider the problem of developing economies and peace as the two basic issues which demand our constant and resolute attention.

In order for the Movement of Nonaligned Countries to meet its historic objectives; in order for it to stand up to colonialism and imperialism; in order to have the moral strength to demand that states party to international military pacts—the result of contradictions between social systems—find an adequate peaceful framework to solve their differences, it is imperative that the differences within the Movement itself be solved promptly and justly. It is likewise indispensable to systematically establish and promote cooperation in the economic and political fields among all member countries of the Movement, as a safeguard against external machinations and as a starting point for international cooperation.

Unity is more imperative than ever. As chair of the Movement, we have explored solutions to the problems in Southwest Asia and we have acted and will continue to act as mediator to promote the peaceful solution to the differences arising out of the military conflict between Iraq and Iran. Other less urgent problems have received our attention. We thank the coordinating bureau and all the member countries for the help they have given us in meeting our obligations as the country presiding over the Movement.

On this historic occasion, the Movement's 20th anniversary, allow us, as temporary head of the Movement, to mention what the Nonaligned Movement has represented for our own country.

In September 1961, we had just reaffirmed our sovereignty through the people's heroism in the sands of Playa Girón [Bay of Pigs]. We joined the Movement as a socialist and underdeveloped country. We have always tried to fully meet our obligations as a member of this community motivated by a program that has had our support, and we will continue to do so, in the future. But what we would like to stress the most now is Cuba's gratitude to the Movement of Nonaligned Countries for the firm and constant support it has given to our continuous struggle against attempts to undermine our national sovereignty. In 1961, the Belgrade Declaration stated that the naval base on Guantánamo, illegally maintained by the United States against the will of our people, was a threat to Cuba's sovereignty and territorial integrity. Since then, our country has never lacked the support of the nonaligned for the recovery of that usurped portion of our land and for other battles we have had to wage against the same adversary.

Cuba will never forget this solidarity.

Mr Chairman and esteemed members, great tasks imply great responsibilities. And great responsibilities demand great decisions. Through its summit conferences the Movement has been inspired to struggle for lofty principles which guide us even now in the face of difficult international circumstances. The path of these 20 years shows us that the future belongs to the cause of peace, national independence and development, which we have taken in our hands. The increase during this period of countries that today form part of the Nonaligned Movement is the result of successive victories over the oppressive forces of the colonial past and the neocolonialist present which we set out to defeat in 1961. In that broad historic period in which Algeria consolidated its independence, we also find the collapse of Portuguese colonialism and the incorporation of Mozambique, Guinea-Bissau, Cape Verde and São Tomé and Principe, completed later on with Angola's independence. The heroic lesson given by Vietnam that, regardless how mighty an imperialist power may be, it cannot dominate a people, no matter how small, that is determined to be free. Zimbabwe, that gained independence through the heroic battles of its people, allows us to anticipate the future victory of Namibia and the disappearance of the hateful apartheid in South Africa. The Palestinian people, who have tirelessly continued their determined struggle to recover their stolen territories and to form their own nation-state, received the constant support of the Movement and of all progressive forces which have made the just cause of the PLO one of the essential demands of this period. Many other countries in Africa and Asia attained independence through liberation processes or made decisive revolutionary changes.

In addition to Panama's recovery of its sovereignty over its Canal Zone, Latin America contributed to the revolutionary processes that enabled Grenada to begin decisive transformations and Nicaragua to become one of the most significant examples today of the struggle for democracy and national freedom in the Americas.

Struggle has been the peoples' instrument for those victories which have enriched and strengthened the Movement of Non-aligned Countries. We must have this same readiness to energetically defend our program and our principles to guarantee the future success of the ambitious goals we have set for ourselves.

Unity is at the very foundation of our common action.

If we want to be worthy of our twenty-year history, the New Delhi meeting should be a time of unity and reaffirmation. You are meeting under the inspiration of the memory of that eminent representative of the cause of national independence and peace, Jawaharlal Nehru, and the presence of Indira Gandhi, the heir to that beautiful tradition and prominent personality of the Movement and the entire international community. India's contribution to the establishment of the principles guiding our Movement and its permanent contribution to its unity provide the proper framework that can make the New Delhi meeting exceptionally important in the process of consolidating our Movement.

I firmly believe that in this, the year of its 20th anniversary, the Movement of Nonaligned Countries will prove the historic validity of our principles and the strength of our organization.

Fidel Castro Ruz
Havana
February 4, 1981

The struggle for dignity

Esteemed Prime Minister Indira Gandhi; Distinguished heads of state or government; Members of the delegations; Distinguished Guests:

On the morning of September 9, 1979, at the closing of the Sixth Summit Conference in Havana after many hours of work together with the heads of state or government who are members of the Movement and after long and not always quiet debates—which at times seemed to threaten our cohesion—I ended my closing address with these heartfelt words: "We can say that our Movement is more united than ever! Our Movement is more vigorous than ever! Our Movement is more powerful than ever! Our Movement is more independent than ever! Our Movement is more ours than ever!"

Today, after a term of more than three years, upon handing over the Chair of the Movement of Nonaligned Countries to our esteemed Indira Gandhi and to India, which she so rightfully represents upon the basis of historic merit, we can state, as testimony of having fulfilled a duty, that the unity of our Movement has not been weakened, that its vigor has grown, that its independence has been safeguarded against all plots intended to curtail it. It is a Movement fully belonging to a community of countries which throughout 22 years of joint efforts have made it an instrument for peace, national liberation and economic development.

The following speech by Fidel Castro was presented as out-going chair at the Seventh Summit Conference of the Movement of Nonaligned Countries in New Delhi, India. The book prepared by Cuba for the summit to which Fidel Castro refers is "The World Economic and Social Crisis."

si nos
imponen
la guerra
¡PELEAREMOS!

°Why punish Cuba? Is it because our country, with modest resources but with a deep sense of social justice, has given man dignity like never before and has met his needs for education, health care, culture, employment and well-being? Is it because Cuba remains unremittingly loyal to the revolutionary movement, to the principle of solidarity among the peoples, to the staunch and determined struggle against colonialism, neocolonialism, fascism and racism?°

We all know that it has not been an easy task. Never before had the Movement been subjected to so much external pressure nor had it faced the serious internal problems which have recently threatened to weaken our unity.

During the Sixth Summit Conference, the controversial interpretations of the developments in Kampuchea had already prevented unanimity. The just consensus reached then, that is, that Kampuchea's seat remain vacant, was not accepted as legitimate by all member countries. Three years later, and in a less controversial atmosphere, ratification of that consensus has been necessary to fully vindicate the justness of the decision made then by Cuba.

The positions announced by Kampuchea and Vietnam after the meeting of the three countries of former Indochina—in our view—provide the prospects for attaining a solution of the dispute that is acceptable to all. We very sincerely hope so, although Cuba's solidarity with heroic Vietnam, Laos and the new Kampuchea is well known and I must very frankly say so.

Shortly after the Havana conference, developments in Afghanistan caused new commotion within our ranks. What some viewed simply as an expression of the Afghan people's right to request solidarity assistance to be protected from external aggressions that were rekindling and manipulating the internal conflict, others viewed as an unacceptable intervention.

Practically in the same area and at the same time and in spite of our joint efforts with other heads of state to prevent it, the Iran–Iraq conflict broke out, confronting two important and respected members of the Movement in a hitherto irreconcilable war, shaking the very foundations of our necessary cohesion.

More recently, the Organization of African Unity, which rallied Africa's efforts after the collapse of colonialism, encountered difficulties which, for different reasons, have lately prevented it from holding its meetings, and only very recently does it seem to be overcoming them.

This hasty outline of events which have enabled imperialism to continue its constant attempts at disbanding and destroying this Movement that opposes its policies and challenges it hegemony, shows that although the struggle against the forces threatening peace, the remnants of colonialism and imperialism's still undefeated might is never an easy task, it is rendered even more difficult and hazardous if we are to wage such a battle with our forces split by disunity.

Hence, while continuing our efforts for peace and our constant struggle for independence and development during these three years, we deemed it necessary more than once to draw the attention of the Movement to the urgent task of rebuilding our unity and healing our own wounds.

We do not wish to tire the heads of state or government with a detailed review of our work during this period. They and their delegations have at their disposal a written report which contains our detailed rendering of accounts. In this speech I will limit myself to fundamental questions.

Prior to the December 1979 events, anticipating that contradictions between the Afghan revolution and some of its neighbors threatened to obstruct our unity, we made the necessary efforts with all parties concerned to impede a sharpening of the conflict and future complications. We centered our efforts on Afghanistan and Pakistan. During the Sixth Summit Conference in Havana we succeeded in arranging a meeting between the two illustrious statesmen of the two nations, since we felt that if an agreement was reached between them, the necessary conditions would then be created for a satisfactory return to political normality in the area and the furthering of friendly relations between Afghanistan and all its neighbors. We also made similar efforts with representatives from other countries in the area. We pursued these objectives despite Cuba's sympathy for and solidarity with the Afghan revolution, which we have never failed to express nor have we ever concealed. We did not achieve the necessary success. Thus, when the events involving the presence of Soviet troops in Afghanistan occurred, we decided to continue following the road we had embarked upon previously in the quest for an honorable and acceptable settlement for all parties involved in the complex situation that had arisen. Through the Cuban minister of foreign affairs and other leaders we established the necessary contacts and formalized these efforts. But conditions were not ripe then for fruitful results.

Afterwards, when we realized that the mediation efforts of the UN secretary-general through the Under Secretary, Mr Diego Cordovés, could advance in an already more favorable climate, we discontinued our efforts and supported the UN endeavors which we all hope will produce promising results that will undoubtedly be of great value for our Movement's cohesion and integrity.

Regarding the Iran–Iraq conflict, in which we also tried to mediate from the very beginning, we have kept the members of the Movement informed about the steps taken by the group chaired by Cuba and made up by India, Zambia and the Palestine Liberation Organization, which was specially organized for that purpose by mandate of the [1981] New Delhi meeting.

The Nonaligned Movement has not been alone in this endeavor. The efforts made by Olof Palme on behalf of the United Nations' secretary-general and by the Islamic representatives, made up by heads of state or government, coincided with those of the Movement. The activities of the Nonaligned committee and Cuba are contained in the document that has been distributed. The fact that it has not been possible so far to reach a satisfactory agreement for the parties regrettably indicates the bitterness characterizing that conflict. But we must not be discouraged. I am certain that the conference will avail itself of the presence here of the heads of delegations of Iraq and Iran to take new steps along the path toward the necessary conciliation.

The prolongation of the war involving the country which we had unanimously agreed at the Sixth Summit Conference to entrust with the task of organizing the Seventh Conference, endangered the continuity of our meetings. When it became evident that the conflict would not end before the date set for the Seventh Summit Conference, I decided, with the support and encouragement of other heads of state or government, to undertake actions to facilitate an honorable and just solution to this difficult question.

The constructive attitude of Iraq, and specially of its president, Saddam Hussein, in accepting the proposed solution with great understanding and responsibility—which deserves the Movement's gratitude—allowed for us to provide the world with a proof of the unity, solidarity and inherent strength of the Movement of Nonaligned Countries. Furthermore, we should express our gratitude to Iraq and its president for the careful arrangements they made to host the Seventh Summit Conference. Hence, it is not surprising that in the consultations we made concerning the adoption of the change in venue with the acquiescence of the heads of state or government, while unanimously endorsing India as the new venue, the majority of them, acknowledging Iraq's unselfish attitude, accepted the Iraqi wishes for Baghdad to have priority as the possible venue for the Eighth Summit Conference, a decision that must be made at this august meeting.

I believe I voice the common feelings of the heads of state or government in reiterating here our gratitude to the government of India and its prime minister, Indira Gandhi, for her prompt and determined response to the Movement's request to assume—on such short notice—the task of organizing the Seventh Summit Conference. India has welcomed us with hospitality and affection, thus confirming the stand it has maintained since the days when Jawaharlal Nehru contributed to the founding of our Movement with his creative ideas. India's great traditions, its struggle against colonialism and imperialism, for independence, development and peace, have earned it prestige in world politics that at the service of our Movement, increases its strength. The names of Gandhi and Nehru are respected and admired throughout the world. India's maturity, perseverance and good judgment in the quest for reasonable and peaceful solutions to the problems of our times, its unrestricted adherence to the basic principles of the Nonaligned Movement, guarantee that under Indira Gandhi's wise leadership, the Nonaligned Countries will continue advancing in their unrenounceable role as bulwarks of peace, national independence and development, strengthen their cohesion and unity and continue honorably fulfilling the difficult duties imposed on us by these critical times.

I cannot summarize our actions during this term without expressing my gratitude to the heads of state or government. I have received all necessary support on their part. I was able to count with consensus in every case, not to say unanimity. The response concerning the change of venue could not have been more prompt nor full. This proves that differences in political systems or concepts are compatible among us, with full coincidence on the principles that guide over our actions.

This unity is ever more urgent for us.

When we met in Havana we already noted the threats to world peace and the onslaughts against the vulnerable economies of the underdeveloped countries, but we were far from imagining that only a few months later the world situation was to become even more somber, and that the world's political and economic prospects would be even more risky and bitter.

It is not an apocalyptic vocation that makes us believe that the world has never been so close to a catastrophe that, because of its nuclear nature, tends to be definitive and that never before have hunger, backwardness, ignorance and disease affected so many millions of human beings.

The dangers of war already existing when we met in 1979 increased very rapidly when the new president of the United States decided to impose, as a condition for peace, the acceptance of his country's military supremacy and that of the alliance it leads. The disruption of détente—a threat which we all stood up against during the days of the Sixth Summit Conference—became an inauspicious factor in the new international political situation. The growing arms buildup we rejected in Havana reappeared vigorously and in 1982 annual military spending reached unprecedented figures. The threat of filling Europe with missiles and turning it into the local scenario for the beginning of a terrible world drama, gained new momentum.

I am certain that we are all aware that in this New Delhi meeting the most urgent task for us is to immediately put at the service of peace all the forces we represent in world politics, wherein we account for the majority of the countries of the international community. We must make the big nuclear powers pledge that none will be the first to use that devastating weapon. We must demand from the main protagonists of a possible nuclear confrontation, from the representatives of the powerful military pacts that presently oppose each other worldwide, to abandon all ideas of supremacy, to immediately start the negotiations humanity clamors for, to accept military balance at the lowest possible levels, as the threshold for universal and complete disarmament, the sole and definitive guarantee against war.

The danger of war threatens us as citizens of the world, but it also affects us as peoples that aspire to reaffirm or conquer, whatever the case may be, our national independence and develop our battered economies. The very same policy that is inspired in the senseless pretentions of military supremacy is the one that creates situations in the Middle East, southern Africa and Central America, against which the Movement has had to raise its voice during the years that I am reporting on to this summit meeting.

We were all horrified and shocked by the Dantesque sight of the warmongering invasion of southern Lebanon, and the treacherous aggression against Syria, the genocidal attack against Beirut and the cruel slaughters in Sabra and Shatila. The heroic attitude of the Palestinian fighters and of the Lebanese patriots and their unequalled courage aroused admiration throughout the world. Never before had the Palestinian cause seemed so just than in contrast with the repulsive brutality of its adversaries. Humanity shall never forget the heroism of those subject to aggression nor the barbarity of the aggressors. It is indeed dramatic that the Hebrew people, who aroused universal compassion and sympathy when Hitler threatened to exterminate them, are now being led by

Zionism to become engaged in that insane genocide. This explains why in Israel itself a clamor for peace and a demand for the punishment of those responsible for the killings have been raised.

But all of this could not have been possible if the Israeli aggressors had not received their weapons from a world imperialist center all of us identify that made this crime possible. The execrable adventurism of the Begins and Sharons exists solely as a result of a repulsive and confessed strategic alliance between Israel and the United States.

In the face of such a tragic massacre, the Movement could not be an impassive bystander. With the support of all heads of state or government, we appealed to world public opinion, on whose behalf Cuba acted in the UN Security Council and in the General Assembly.

Following my instructions as President of the Movement, the Cuban minister of foreign affairs, comrade Isidoro Malmierca, carried to the besieged Beirut the Nonaligned Countries' message of solidarity.

The Palestinian tragedy has served to confirm the support, not only of the Movement of Nonaligned Countries, but of other important forces of the international community the world over, for the Palestinian cause represented by the PLO, the Palestinians' right to return to their lands, their exercise of full self-determination, the establishment of an independent state, and the recognition of the PLO as the sole and legitimate representative of its people. I am convinced that the conference will serve to reaffirm this universal demand with all the necessary strength.

As we expected, in southern Africa it was necessary to extend permanent solidarity with the Namibian people and their representative organization, SWAPO. The government in Pretoria is competing with that of Israel to become one of the most ominous factors in world politics. It does not confine itself to exploit, discriminate against and oppress the 20 million Africans in the so-called Republic of South Africa; it is not satisfied with obstinately opposing the independence of Namibia; but also, in order to preserve its domination over southern Africa, it threatens, exerts pressure upon, blackmails and attacks the Front Line States and other neighboring countries, striving through the use of terror to prevent them from justly supporting the South African and Namibian patriots so heroically fighting for their rights and liberation. While continuing to support UNITA in Angola, and the counterrevolutionaries they have armed and are operating in

Mozambique, they have now shamelessly and directly attacked Angola and Mozambique and launched retaliatory raids against a small and defenseless country such as Lesotho. The South African Nazi-racists' hands reached the Seychelles, in an adventure whereby their mercenaries and troops attempted to overthrow the progressive government of that sovereign and nonaligned state.

Namibia did not lack the Movement's growing support during the three-year period under examination. We also expressed our militant solidarity with Angola, Mozambique, Lesotho, Zimbabwe and Zambia. However, when condemning the South African leaders, we all knew that their actions would not be possible without the protection, aid and encouragement of the United States. The Movement condemned the U.S. vetoes that allowed South Africa to elude international sanctions. And we are certain that the Seventh Summit Conference will also condemn the United States' attempt to link the necessary and unpostponable departure of South African troops from Namibia—where they remain in violation of the decisions and principles of the international community—with the presence of Cuban internationalist troops in Angola, summoned there by its legitimate government, with the support and endorsement of the Fifth Summit Conference of Colombo, to defend the territorial integrity of the Angolan nation.

The United States government has systematically attempted, through successive high-level missions, to exert pressure on Angola and the other Front Line States supporting it, to accept the false thesis of "linkage." On every occasion, they have met categorical rejection. Angola and Cuba, in the statement signed by their ministers of foreign affairs in February, 1982, declared that Namibia's full independence, through the total and unconditional withdrawal of South African troops and the ceasing of all aggressions and threats against Angola, would create the conditions, so that in exercising their sovereign rights, Angola and Cuba would decide upon the gradual withdrawal of the Cuban troops in the time schedule agreed upon. Needless to say, Cuba—on whose behalf I ask for your permission to speak now—will always accept Angola's sovereign decision unhesitatingly.

The Movement of Nonaligned Countries can feel pleased that in these three trying years for the peoples of southern Africa, years of constant pressures on Namibia and brutal actions by South Africa, that SWAPO, the Front Line States and the African National Congress—which leads the struggle of millions of blacks

91

who are discriminated against and oppressed in South Africa against apartheid—have not lacked the active solidarity of the nonaligned countries.

In condemning South Africa, we have never forgotten that its rulers are supported by the United States, which considers it a strategic factor in the policy it seeks to impose. We have not forgotten either that South Africa holds a privileged position in the economic, technological and military cooperation it receives, not only from the United States, but also from other Western countries. We are certain that the Seventh Summit will reaffirm this traditional policy of the Movement.

U.S. aggression against Libya, which has led the United States to perpetrate true acts of war against that member country, creates a new danger zone in Africa and elicits our strongest protest.

When examining these African problems in the summit conference, the representatives of the Democratic Saharawi Arab Republic will not be among us. Their absence is one of the results of discrepancies within the OAU. This is another matter on which I am aware that there are differences of opinion. However, as far as Cuba is concerned, I cannot but express that the Democratic Saharawi Arab Republic and the Polisario Front have our sympathy and our solidarity, and we expect their prompt incorporation into the Movement, since we consider their cause to be absolutely just.

During these three years under review, Central America has also become a danger spot for world peace and a center of death and possible military aggressions.

At the Sixth Summit Conference we welcomed the Sandinistas —who had defeated Somoza—as brothers happily joining our task. Yet, the ominous and senseless policy of those who have increased the universal danger of war attempts to turn Central America and the Caribbean into a scenario of East-West contradictions. The idea is to make the world believe that what happened in Nicaragua and what is happening in El Salvador and Guatemala is not the result of decades of growing protest and of uninterrupted struggles in which the hungry peoples, the disdainfully called banana republics, weary of so much tyranny, exploitation and humiliation, the landless peasants, the hungry and jobless men and women, and even the adolescents who have no schools to go to rise up to clamor for justice, but that all this is rather the consequence of a grim design in which Moscow, through Cuba, would manipulate these peoples.

U.S. intervention in Central America, which began long before the 1917 Soviet Revolution, has persisted since then and antedated the Cuban Revolution by several decades; Yankee support for genocide in El Salvador; collaboration with the Ríos Montt sinister tyranny, similar to that they always provided to the Somoza dynasty. The efforts to use Honduras as a spearhead for U.S. intervention aimed at crushing the Nicaraguan revolution are to be justified with pretexts taken from the arsenal of McCarthyism, already repudiated in the official statements of Mexico, Panama, Venezuela and Colombia.

The Movement of Nonaligned Countries has recently refuted all these deceitful interpretations at the ministerial meeting of the coordinating bureau in Managua, and has unequivocally identified those mainly responsible for the present explosive situation existing in Central America and the Caribbean. The peoples of Central America and the Caribbean favor peace and a negotiated solution, enabling their access to full independence under democratic conditions. A negotiated solution to the continuing bloodshed in El Salvador was proposed by Mexico and France through an irrefutable project. The peaceful negotiation of the regional problems was postulated by the presidents of Mexico and Venezuela and reaffirmed by their foreign ministers and those of Panama and Colombia at the recent meeting held in Contadora Island. This is why the meeting of the Movement in Managua, free of all bias and sectarianism, identified the United States as responsible for the failure of a peaceful solution to the situation in the area.

On the other hand, Cuba has had to strengthen its defense, train an additional half a million citizens as a supplement to the Revolutionary Armed Forces due to the constant provocative threats launched by the president of the United States against our country and echoed in varying keys by the successive secretaries of state, Haig and Shultz, and by the secretary of defense, Weinberger, in terms so precise and threatening that they leave no room for confusion.

The decision of the present U.S. administration to resort to any means whatsoever to punish Cuba is proclaimed openly.

Why punish Cuba? Is it because our country, with modest resources but with a deep sense of social justice, has given man dignity like never before and has met his needs for education, health care, culture, employment and well-being? Is it because Cuba remains unremittingly loyal to the revolutionary movement, to the principle of solidarity among the peoples, to the staunch and determined struggle against colonialism, neocolonialism, fascism and racism? Is it because our country has pursued an unflinching policy of cooperation with the countries of the Third World and has even shed its blood for the just causes of other peoples? Is it because we do not sell out? Is it because we do not betray our principles? Is it because we have not and will never yield to the modern barbarians of our times?

The imperialists are consumed by hatred and impotence in the face of a small, hard-working country, that leads a humble and dignified life, such as Cuba. How to kill an example? How to destroy moral force? How to lower a flag that has already resisted the hostility of seven U.S. administrations?

The illegal and criminal Yankee economic blockade against Cuba has already lasted 23 years, an event unprecedented in the world. The U.S. Guantánamo naval base still exists, with the sole purpose of humiliating our people. U.S. spy planes constantly fly around Cuba and, at times, openly violate our airspace.

And even worse, through reliable sources we have learned that the new U.S. administration has instructed the Central Intelligence Agency to resume the plans to kill Cuban leaders, especially its president. What else could be expected from such an unscrupulous government? And what is there to be surprised about in these cynical imperialist practices? Had not other presidents made similar plans in the past and tried to carry them out on several occasions as was confirmed by the United States Senate itself? However, all attempts will be useless. Our revolution does not rely on men, it relies on ideas and ideas cannot be assassinated.

Although we want peace in the region and we strive for peace, we will not capitulate before threats of any sort. We can assure the Seventh Summit Conferenece that the Salvadoran revolutionaries cannot be militarily defeated; we can express our conviction that Nicaragua will not be forced to yield; and we can categorically say that Cuba may be wiped out, but it will never be intimidated or defeated. As we said 30 years ago: "The island will sink into the sea before we accept being anyone's slaves!"

Dozens of U.S. congressmen have censured the policy of threats and the interventionist designs that have likewise been rejected in successive polls by the vast majority of U.S. citizens.

We are certain that the Movement will further the stands taken during the period we are reporting on in its Seventh Summit Conference.

Our solidarity actions should also embrace small and brave

Grenada, a permanent target of imperialist activity and pressure; the new revolutionary Republic of Surinam, today a victim of mercenary threats, economic blockade, slander campaigns and maneuvers aimed at isolating it; the just demands of the Panamanian government and people to have respected the agreements restoring sovereignty over the Canal territory to Panama; the efforts of Belize to consolidate its independence and preserve its territorial integrity; and the historic demand of Puerto Rico, which is and will be Latin American because of its history, its culture, its language and its geography, where attempts are made to tie it permanently to the colonial government of the United States.

In conformity with the mandate of successive summit conferences, we have defended at the United Nations the right of Puerto Ricans to self-determination and independence, denied to them by the United States. We have no doubt that the Movement will endorse these stands.

Unfortunately, there is a problem in our region which involves two Third World nations. One of them, Guyana, a distinguished member of the Movement and the other, Venezuela, which has expressed the desire to join. We fervently hope and expect that this dispute will be solved by negotiations in keeping with the principles of the nonaligned countries. Working to achieve this end must be our firm objective.

The colonial war waged by Mrs Thatcher and her government against Argentina's right to exercise its territorial sovereignty over the Malvinas, a right that the Movement has acknowledged since its very inception, elicited the nonaligned countries' solidarity with the country under attack. That is why Cuba, despite its political and ideological differences with the Argentine government, did not hesitate to support the just demand of that noble people.

We may inform the member countries that the Malvinas events marked a significant moment in the development of a Latin American consciousness, in the strengthening of the unity of what Cuban poet José Martí called Our America as opposed to "the other America" which he called "the turbulent and brutal North that despises us."

The colonial war in the South Atlantic has been an unforgettable lesson for all Latin Americans. It evidenced, as never before, the true face of U.S. imperialism, its contempt for the interests of Latin America and the neocolonial content it attaches to the hypocritically called Treaty for Reciprocal Assistance on which the security of the hemisphere is allegedly based. This Treaty obliged the United States to join with the Latin American countries for the defense of Argentina's sovereign rights. In ignoring it, Washington joined the European aggressors against Latin America. As a response to the colonialists' identification with one another, the Malvinas episode served to unite the Latin American peoples.

The growing awareness with which the governments and political forces of the region rally in the defense of their common economic interests, the search for Latin American solutions to Latin American problems and the growing tendency by the countries in the region to join the Movement of Nonaligned Countries, leaving behind the imperial orbit that retained them, are both a hope for future struggles and the best tribute to Simón Bolívar, the continental liberator, and to José Martí, the Cuban National Hero, whose 200th and 130th anniversaries, respectively we shall celebrate in 1983, as our great common heritage.

The resumption of the democratic process in Bolivia is also an expression of the positive changes taking place in Latin America.

There are other danger zones.

The Indian Ocean—to which U.S. strategists have attached decisive importance since they consider that its link with a major world oil-producing region makes it their own unrenounceable zone—has witnessed an increased concentration of military and naval troops in its waters and adjoining territories. The strategic Diego García enclave, usurped from Mauritius, is being expanded as a naval base of the United States, which is also arranging to build new military bases in countries which, because of their links with our Movement, should have rejected the use of their territories for these purposes.

The Movement of Nonaligned Countries has systematically demanded that the Indian Ocean be declared a zone of peace. It has called for the withdrawal from its waters of all naval forces not belonging to bordering countries. The Coastal States' Conference on the Indian Ocean should have already been held, but it has been postponed to 1984 due to obstacles put in its way by the United States. The Movement has and should continue to come out in favor of the immediate holding of this conference and support the important initiative presented by the president of Madagascar, Didier Ratsiraka, to hold a meeting of the heads of state in the area for this same purpose.

In this summary of our activities, we would like to state that the Movement in all international forums and in all its meetings during these three years has reiterated its support for the Democratic

People's Republic of Korea against all threats as well as its support for the necessary unification of the Korean nation, divided only to meet the interests of imperialism.

Moreover, our solidarity has been constant toward another small country, also divided and occupied. Respect for the unity, territorial integrity and nonaligned status of Cyprus continues to be the position of the Movement of Nonaligned Countries.

We have been able to observe how regional situations that threaten many developing countries, most of which are members of our Movement, are interrelated—at times quite arbitrarily—to situations involving worldwide warmongering policies and dangers of conflict. The very same people who turn military superiority into a prerequisite for negotiations; the very same people who attempt to turn Europe, dozens of times devastated by war, into another territory planted with nuclear missiles; the very same people who raise their military budgets at the expense of their peoples' social security, education, medical care, and international development assistance, are those who establish strategic alliances with Israel, build up that country and make it more arrogant and self-confident; who ally themselves with South Africa in order to act on the continent to further their economic interests and military strategy; who, in order to perpetuate their exploitation and control over Central America and the Caribbean, intentionally distort the drama resulting from the poverty and backwardness of those peoples, presenting it as part of the East-West conflict.

For that reason, we have said that for us, the members of the Movement of Nonaligned Countries, to fight against war does not only mean opposing universal holocaust, but also defending our own immediate political interests. There is an additional reason, as important as the above, which impels us toward a concrete and immediate struggle for peace and détente. We are all convinced that without peace, development is not possible, just as peace would not be possible without development. As long as $650 billion are invested in weapons every year and such spending is growing at such a rate that it will reach over $1,500 billion by 1990, amounting to an accumulated total of over $15,000 billion in the next 20 years—according to conservative estimates we have made—the international financial requirements for development cannot be met. Warmongering policies lead to considering our wealth as part of the strategic reserves; seeing our coasts as elements of international geopolitics; attempting to gain, through flattery or imposition, the acquiescence of our governments to the policies to be adopted at international forums. The danger of war permeates and undermines everything: national independence, economic sovereignty, development prospects.

For that reason, if the survival of humanity, now at risk, would not lead us to brandish the banner of peace as the very core of the stand of the Movement of Nonaligned Countries our pressing economic needs would also lead us to defend peace as our first and most immediate demand.

The world's economic situation has contributed to worsening further the poverty and backwardness of the so-called Third World countries, rendering their aspirations for development more unattainable in the near future.

In my speech representing the Movement at the 34th Session of the United Nations General Assembly and in other international forums such as the Interparliamentary Union and the World Federation of Trade Unions, I have, in general terms, dealt with the serious economic and social problems affecting the Third World, their causes and possible solutions.

It would be impossible to convey to the Seventh Summit Conference, in detail, the dramatic panorama from a scientific examination of the world economy. I have found it useful, however, to elaborate on those concerns, reflections and ideas I have advanced in recent years by making, with the invaluable assistance of a group of Cuban economists, a systematic presentation of the world's economic and social crisis and its deep effects on underdeveloped countries. The book resulting from that effort is a compendium and an examination of thousands of loose data from publications of the most prestigious international organizations and specialized journals, which in my view may be a useful tool for our immediate work.

It is in this spirit and with all modesty that I am submitting it to the heads of state or government and all those attending the conference. Its pages bring out a diagnosis that might be familiar to us all but which we have not always been able to back with the hard statistics as such. I am certain that many will find in this book an exact portrait of the distressing difficulties they face today.

Unquestionably, the world is undergoing one of the worst economic crises in its history.

This crisis has most severely affected the underdeveloped countries and indeed, its effects have been worse in these countries than in any other area in the world. This holds true particularly for the oil-importing underdeveloped countries whose growth rates, which had averaged 5.6 percent from 1970 to 1980, dropped to 1.4 percent in 1981 and were probably lower in 1982.

A decisive factor in that development was the drop in commodity prices since late 1980.

The prices for sugar, coffee, cocoa, tea, palm oil, coconut oil, sisal, cotton, aluminium and practically all commodities have dropped notably.

Even oil prices, which started to decline in late 1981 as a result of the crisis, have fallen faster in recent weeks among other things due to the policies of British and Norwegian firms which have unleashed a real price war.

It has been estimated that, in comparision to 1980 values, the losses experienced by the oil-importing underdeveloped countries in two years alone—1981 and 1982—amount to some $29 billion.

With the decline in commodity prices and the continuing high prices for manufactured goods and oil, the inevitable result is the worsening unequal exchange affecting most of the Third World.

To illustrate this phenomenon of growing and unjust unequal exchange between developed and underdeveloped countries, including the incidence of oil prices, here are some examples:

In 1960, 6.3 tons of oil could be purchased with the sale of a ton of sugar. In 1982 only 0.7 tons of oil could be bought with the same amount of sugar.

In 1960, 37.3 tons of fertilizers could be bought for a ton of coffee. In 1982 only 15.8 tons could be bought with the same amount of coffee.

In 1959, with the income from the sale of 6 tons of jute fibre, a 7–8 ton truck could be purchased. By late 1982, 26 tons of jute fibre were needed to buy that same truck.

In 1959, with the income from the sale of one ton of copper wire, 39 X-ray tubes for medical purposes could be purchased. By late 1982, only 3 X-ray tubes could be bought with that same ton.

These terms of trade are repeated in most of our export commodities.

This is coupled with the growing protection of Western markets against exports from the Third World. Added to the traditional tariff barriers there is now a wide range of non-tariff barriers.

It is not surprising, under these conditions, to see the extraordinary increase in the underdeveloped world's external debt, which in 1982 surpassed the $600,000 million figure and, at the present rate, according to econometric projections, will reach the incredible figure of $1,473 billion by 1990.

But amortization problems have worsened also with the accelerated growth in debt servicing. The high interest rates irresponsibly and unilaterally established by the United States, out of selfish national economic objectives, directly affected the Third World, whose external debt servicing reached, by late 1982, the impressive figure of some $131 billion.

The situation is such that underdeveloped countries are forced to incur debts with the sole purpose of meeting the obligations of the debt itself.

This huge debt, which drains the underdeveloped countries' export earnings, without the countervailing flow of real resources for development, is in itself conclusive evidence of the irrationality and inequity of the present international economic order.

The underdeveloped world's agricultural output is also facing a serious crisis today. The accelerated population growth, coupled with the growing deterioration of soil fertility and losses resulting from erosion, desertification and other forms of degradation, forecast even greater difficulties by the end of the century.

If the current average of less than 0.4 hectares of agricultural land per Third World inhabitant is insufficient, by the year 2000 this ratio will be less than 0.2 hectares.

From 1975 to 1980, per capita world food production grew at the very low rate of 0.3 percent yearly. That of the developed capitalist countries was 8 percent in 10 years. On the other hand, over 70 underdeveloped countries have witnessed a net decline in per capita food production.

In order to maintain a minimum of food needed, underdeveloped countries have had to increase their yearly imports. In 1980 alone, import values amounted to $52.3 billion.

Over eight years have elapsed since the World Food Conference in Rome (1974), urgently convened in view of the massive famines and alarming decrease of food reserves recorded during those years. On that occasion, the conference solemnly declared that hunger and malnutrition should be wiped off the face of the earth in 10 years and called on all nations to cooperate in an enormous effort to guarantee world food supplies.

The total failure of these endeavors to achieve the basic and essential objective of supplying all human beings with enough food to develop their potentialities for enjoying a full life is today more evident than ever.

Industrialization is a decisive process for the Third World's economic development. Unquestionably, it is equivalent, in strategic terms, to laying the main technological and material base for development. The classical model that postulates that agriculture and raw materials are specialized enough for the underdeveloped countries, leaving industrial production in the hands of the developed countries, does nothing but try to perpetuate a model which our countries firmly reject as irrational, unequal and unjust.

UNIDO itself predicts that, if the present trends are maintained, the underdeveloped countries—with over 80 percent of the world population—will be contributing only 13.5 percent of world industrial production in the year 2000.

The claims made as to the supposedly positive contribution transnationals may make toward the development of the Third World countries are not new.

The underdeveloped countries are offered a transnationalized development model, which would turn them into "export platforms" of manufactured products for the world market.

The results of such transnational industrial development are proven in the following data:

In the 1970s, for every new dollar invested in all the underdeveloped countries, transnationals repatriated approximately $2.2 to their home countries. In the specific case of U.S. transnationals, during 1970–1979 they invested $11 billion and repatriated profits ammounting to $48 billion which means a $4.25 return from the Third World for every new dollar invested in that period.

Obviously, Third World industrialization cannot be the sorry by-product left by the transnationals in exchange for the brutal exploitation of the underdeveloped countries' labor resources, the depletion of their natural resources and the pollution of their territories.

It has been rightfully said that true development should be measured not by growth rates but rather by what has been termed the "quality of life." But, when we attempt to measure factors that would indicate the quality of life, the picture we observe regarding the future of the underdeveloped countries appears even more impressive.

In 1980, three out of every four inhabitants of our planet lived in the underdeveloped world. In view of its present growth trend, from 1990 onwards, there will be 95 million additional inhabitants in the underdeveloped countries every year. From now until the year 2000, in the underdeveloped world as a whole the population will grow at a rate that is three times faster than that of the developed world. That is, more than 90 percent of the total population growth in the period up to the year 2000 will occur in our countries.

Until recently, the year 2000 seemed an indicator of a distant future of unforeseeable events. But, two-thirds of the world population in the year 2000 are already living in today's world; the infant population born each day in our countries will comprise the overwhelming majority of the adults by that time; the children who in the year 2000 will be under 15 will be born just two years from now.

Whatever efforts are made today to protect them, to prevent their death and illness, to provide them with food, housing, medicine, clothing and education, will shape the basic human qualities of that decisive percentage of the future population of the planet. And yet, in view of the present trends, what sort of world will we hand over to those children? What sort of life lies ahead for those 5 billion mouths that have to be fed in the countries of our underdeveloped world, those 5 billion bodies that have to be clothed, shod and sheltered, those 5 billion minds that will strive for knowledge, those 5 billion human beings who will struggle for a decent life, worthy at least of the human condition? What will their quality of life be like?

By the year 2000, in the developed countries as a whole, the annual average per capita gross national product will amount to almost $8,500, while in the underdeveloped countries it will remain under $590. The value of per capita gross production, which in 1975 was 11 times lower for the underdeveloped world than for the developed world, will be 14 times lower by the year 2000, thereby increasing the inferiority gap. Our countries will be poorer.

At their current growth rates, the poorest countries would need 2000–4000 years to bridge the gap separating them from the present level of the most developed capitalist countries.

The food situation is another index of the quality of life with the greatest negative impact on underdeveloped countries.

According to recent FAO data, 40 million people—half of whom are children—die every year from hunger and malnutrition. If we were to decide to keep a minute of silence for every person who died in 1982 owing to hunger-related causes we would not be able to celebrate the advent of the 21st century because we would still have to remain silent.

In 1975, in 80 underdeveloped countries, over 10 percent of the population were undernourished. In 49 of them, this figure was over 15 percent. As we have said, while each year tens of millions of people literally starve to death in the poorest countries, health statistics from the developed capitalist countries reveal the continuous growth—among the highest-income population strata—in the incidence of illnesses deriving at least partially from an excessive food intake.

While future projections differ, they are all equally grim. The FAO, for example, estimates that 10 years from now 150 million human beings will join those who are currently suffering from hunger and malnutrition. For its part, the World Bank estimates that the number of undernourished will rise from 600 million in the mid-'70s to the incredible number of 1.3 billion in the year 2000.

UNICEF foresees that in the year 2000 one out of every five children in the world will be malnourished.

While in the developed countries life expectancy at birth ranges from 72 to 74 years, in the underdeveloped world this does not surpass 55 years. In the countries in Central and Western Africa, life expectancy fluctuates from 42 to 44 years. While in the developed countries full maturity is attained at the age of 45, in other nations this is the most it can be hoped to live.

According to World Health Organization data, infant mortality—fluctuating from 10 to 20 deaths per 1000 live births in the developed countries as a whole in 1981—amounted, in the group of the poorest countries, to a figure ten times higher.

UNICEF has stated this reality graphically and dramatically: of the 122 million children born in 1980—declared by the international community as International Year of the Child—12 million (one out of ten) died before the end of 1981, 95 percent of them in underdeveloped countries.

During their first year of life, 9 out of 10 children in the poorest countries are never given the most elementary health services, much less are they vaccinated against the most common childhood diseases.

The executive director of UNICEF has said that in 1981 the cost of a child's life would be less than $100 annually. If judiciously spent in favor of every single one of the 500 million poorest children of the world, this sum would have covered basic health assistance, elementary education, care during pregnancy and dietary improvement, and would have ensured hygienic conditions and water supply for them. In practice, it turned out to be too high a price for the world community. That is why, in 1981, every two seconds a child paid that price with his life.

Malaria kills one million children a year in the African continent. Nevertheless, it is estimated that the world cost of malaria campaigns would only amount to $2 billion per annum, that is, a sum that is equivalent to what mankind invests in military expenditures every 36 hours.

The phenomenon of unemployment and underemployment is another of the serious problems of the present social situation of the underdeveloped countries.

According to recent ILO estimates, the total amount of chronically unemployed and underemployed in the Third World is over 500 million, a figure equivalent to 50 percent of the economically active population.

It is paradoxical that in a world where there is so much poverty and where the most basic needs of millions of human beings remain unmet, man's productive capacity cannot be fully used.

Moreover, it is in these countries pressed by poverty that 98 percent of the 51 million children under 15 who work in the world is concentrated, generally under conditions of extreme exploitation and lacking all rights.

If the children of our countries starve to death, if their health is unprotected, if they lack shelter, if they cannot work when they become adolescents, what could be the level of education for them in their precarious existence?

UNESCO estimates that in 1980 there were 814 million illiterate adults in the world, most of them in the underdeveloped countries. In the 1960's, a period of sudden upsurge in science and knowledge, the number of people who could not read and write increased by 100 million.

According to UNESCO data, 48 percent of the adult population in the underdeveloped countries is illiterate. Ten underdeveloped countries alone account for 425 million illiterates. In 23 of the poorest countries, over 70 percent of their adult population cannot read or write.

We do not wish to tire you by insisting on this drama. To summarize it, we have included a chart in our book that may give both a sinister and realistic picture of the underdeveloped world.

In the Third World there are:

Hungry	+500 million
Life expectancy under 60	1.7 billion
Lacking medical care	1.5 billion
Living in extreme poverty	+1 billion

Unemployed and underemployed in the underdeveloped world	+500 million
Annual per capita income under $150	800 million
Illiterate adults	814 million
Children lacking or unable to attend school	+200 million
Lacking permanent and adequate water sources	2 billion

How much will these figures have risen to in the next 20 years?

It is up to us to find a solution to this dramatic situation. Proof that a large part of these basic public health, education and other social problems can be solved is the case of our country — if, together with deep structural changes, just economic relations are established among developed and underdeveloped countries, such as our relations within the socialist community.

Cuba—in spite of underdevelopment, of the brutal economic blockade imposed by the United States for more than 20 years, and of the relations of unequal exchange affecting part of its foreign trade combined with other problems related to that part of our economy dependent on relations with the developed capitalist world—has made remarkable progress in just a few years in the spheres of public health, education, culture and other basic aspects of our people's lives.

At present our country has 17,026 doctors, a ratio of one per 576 inhabitants; 48 hospital beds per 10,000 people; it has reduced infant mortality to 17.3 per 1,000 live births, a ratio similar to that of many developed countries and better than some; and life expectancy at birth is already 73.5 years.

Vaccination programs against the main communicable diseases cover one hundred percent of the child population. Diseases like poliomyelitis and malaria have been eradicated; the cases of tuberculosis, leprosy, tetanus, whooping cough, diphtheria, typhoid fever and others have been controlled and considerably reduced; and mortality due to acute diarrheic diseases has been reduced to the minimum. Haemorrhagic dengue, which was undoubtedly introduced into our country by Yankee imperialism, along with other animal and plant diseases, was equally eradicated.

Illiteracy, which stood at 30 percent of the population, was eradicated in record time. An overall minimum educational level of Sixth grade has been achieved for most of the population, the average being even higher, and efforts are now being made to raise that minimum to Ninth grade.

One hundred percent of school-age children attend school; over

90 percent finish Ninth grade; 425,000 youth have graduated from technical and professional schools; another 257,000 as teachers, and 155,000 have graduated from the universities. Our present enrollment in higher education is 200,000, in a population of less than 10 million.

Unemployment, racial discrimination, discrimination against women, begging, prostitution, gambling, drugs and shanty towns have all been eradicated.

At present, over 14,000 Cuban civilians, comprising doctors, health-care personnel, teachers, engineers, economists and other technicians, and skilled workers, provide services in more than 30 Third World countries, in most cases free of charge. More than 150,000 Cubans have done internationalist service in the past 10 years.

On the other hand, over 19,000 youths from 80 Third World countries are studying in our country, the foreign scholarship students per inhabitant ratio being higher than that of any other country in the world. This also shows what can be done in the broad and practically unexplored field of cooperation among the countries of the underdeveloped world.

When addressing the UN General Assembly in 1979, to report on the Sixth Summit Conference, I presented what could be considered a set of Third World demands in view of the already worsening situation. There, I also postulated the need for a flow of additional resources to the Third World over the next 10 years of no less than $300 billion in 1977 real values. In the light of the present situation, all of those proposals have become insufficient.

Whenever I reflect on the very grave economic crisis affecting the Third World, on its grim outlook, and I relate it to the arms race unleashed by imperialism, I often wonder: Why does the United States arm itself beyond all apparent logic? Why does it produce not only new nuclear weapon carriers, neutron bombs, new mass extermination weapon systems, new chemical and bacteriological weapons, but also new aircraft carriers, new battleships, new destroyers, new and sophisticated conventional sea, air and land weapons? Why does it establish new rapid deployment forces? Why does it seek for and set up military bases in all continents? Why does it create arsenals in every possible place? Why does it exert pressure on its allies in the developed capitalist countries who participate in the exploitation of the Third World, for them to increase military spending and arm themselves to the teeth? Is it only to fight their adversaries in the Warsaw Treaty? Or is it that imperialism, perhaps aware of the economic and social realities of the underdeveloped countries, foresees a Third World convulsed by the unending poverty, crisis and exploitation that have been imposed on it? Is it preparing itself militarily to impose Yankee law and order, by fighting underdevelopment, hunger, ignorance, squalor, the lack of basic living conditions and the consequent rebellion and disorder it produces, with the bayonets of their soldiers, the guns of their battleships, and the bombs of their planes in order to secure indispensable oil and raw materials?

Such considerable military preparations of a conventional nature are directly aimed at the Third World. If not, what would be the use of many of those war devices?

As we said at the United Nations, bombs may kill the hungry, the sick and the ignorant, but they cannot kill hunger, disease and ignorance.

As can be seen there is a dramatic link between peace and development. With just one third of the $650 billion used every year for military spending and of the $15,000 billion that will be spent in the coming decades, at the present growth rate of these expenditures, there would be more than enough financial resources to solve the problems of the world's economic and social underdevelopment. This would contribute, moreover, to mitigate considerably the economic problems of even the developed capitalist countries.

In the face of the nuclear tragedy threatening us, the drama of underdevelopment and exploitation that oppresses us, and the economic and social crisis that plagues us, there is no place for resignation or accommodation. The only solution in keeping with man's stature is to struggle.

And this is the message I bring upon ceasing in my capacity as chairman of the Movement of Nonaligned Countries.

To struggle!

To struggle tirelessly for peace, improved international relations, a halt to the arms race and a drastic reduction in military spending and to demand that a considerable part of those funds be dedicated to developing the Third World.

To struggle without respite for an end to the unequal exchange that reduces our real export earnings, shifts the cost of the inflation generated in the developed capitalist countries onto our economies, and ruins our peoples.

To struggle against protectionism, that multiplies the tariff and non-tariff barriers and blocks the marketing of our export commodities and manufactured goods.

To struggle for the cancellation of the external debts of the large number of countries which have no real possibilities of paying them and drastically lighten the burden of debt servicing for those that, under new conditions, may be able to fulfill their commitments.

To struggle for emergency measures to halt or compensate the drop in the underdeveloped countries' export earnings and other measures of direct assistance to bring about sound balances of payments.

To struggle to establish a new, equitable, stable and universal international financial and monetary system whose credit and voting options reflect the needs of the various groups and categories of countries rather than the economic power of some of its members; that is capable of acting in a genuinely multilateral sense rather than in response to the pressures exerted by transnational banks or a group of capitalist powers; and that, finally, can respond in the long run in keeping with the magnitude and structural character of the underdeveloped countries' balances of payments.

To struggle, with international support, to draw up plans for each country to meet as far as possible its own basic food needs; to find an immediate solution for the acute deficit in foodstuffs in certain regions of the world, by means of a considerable flow from the large world surpluses transferred in the form of donations, soft credits and sales at special prices; to create an awareness of the inevitable need—if we wish to end rural underemployment, unemployment and hunger—for profound socioeconomic and structural changes, such as agrarian reform, that will make it possible to adopt higher forms of agricultural production; and also, with international cooperation, to promote programs against erosion, desertification, deforestation and other forms of soil deterioration, also protecting the main sources of water in each country.

To struggle for industrialization that responds to our interests, can be integrated with the rest of the economy and paves the way for development; and to keep the transnational corporations and foreign private investments from controlling it and from deforming the Third World industrialization process.

To struggle in each of our countries for the adoption of measures to control and limit the activities of the transnational corporations, fully exercising our right to sovereignty over our resources, including the right to nationalize them.

To struggle resolutely for a stable and definitive solution to the Third World's energy needs, keeping in mind, in addition to oil, the joint use of other renewable sources of energy and the international economic cooperation that is absolutely necessary for their development.

To struggle to ensure—along with the absolutely necessary flow of substantial resources derived from the reduction of military spending—a contribution of financial, technological and human resources that will help solve the complex problems already analyzed. Many countries (including a group of underdeveloped ones) that do not have the required financial means could participate by contributing other resources in line with their possibilities—for example, by sending doctors, engineers, planners, teachers and other technical personnel either free of charge or under favorable payment conditions.

To struggle consistently for a solid, coherent movement of cooperation among the underdeveloped countries.

To struggle to restore and apply the most positive aspects of our demands for a new international economic order, opposing those who attempt to water them down, and continue calling for a process of global negotiations that would serve as a real forum discussing and seeking out solutions to our most pressing problems.

To struggle to make all Third World states aware of the need to promote indispensable internal structural changes and measures aimed at raising the people's standard of living, which are an inseparable part of any real process of development—especially those related to income redistribution, job creation, health, housing and education.

To struggle urgently to tackle the present critical situation of health in the Third World through the massive mobilization of national and international financial and human resources.

To struggle firmly, with the required international assistance, to develop programs to combat illiteracy; to provide schooling for all children; to raise the levels of teaching; to train technicians and skilled personnel on a mass scale; to give our people access to a university education; and to develop the rich, age-old potential of our peoples' cultures, combating all forms of dependence and cultural colonialism and the deformation of our cultures.

To struggle to increase the prestige, authority and role of the United Nations and its specialized agencies; to give them our solid majority support in the struggle for peace and security for all peoples, for a just international order and for a solution to the tragic problem of underdevelopment that adversely affects the vast majority of countries. The existence of such an organization as the United Nations, with growing solidity, influence and power, is increasingly indispensable for the future of the world.

To struggle tenaciously to promote the closest possible unity within the Movement of Nonaligned Countries and among all Third World states. To not allow anybody or anything to divide us. To solve by means of negotiations and political formulas those problems which make some of our countries at times oppose one another. Let us be an indestructible battle line of peoples demanding our noble aspirations, our legitimate interests and our inalienable right to survive, both as Third World countries and as an inseparable part of humanity.

We have never been characterized by resignation, submission or defeatism in the face of difficulties. We have firmly faced complex, difficult situations in the last few years with unity and determination. We have strived together, we have struggled together and together we have scored victories. In this same spirit and with this same determination, we must be ready to wage the most colossal, just, worthy and necessary battle of our peoples' lives and future.

Thank you.

We will stand by our principles

Esteemed Prime Minister Robert Mugabe; Distinguished heads of state or government; Delegates; Distinguished guests:

As we meet today in this militant Africa under the chairmanship of one of its authentic leaders to celebrate the founding 25 years ago in Belgrade of the Movement of Nonaligned Countries, it is evident that the objectives that forced a small group of Third World countries to come together in order to defend principles closely related to their own existence and essential for securing their future, have dramatically survived and remained practically intact during this quarter of a century. The threat of a nuclear war, condemned by the founding countries—which issued a call to avert it through the only and irreplaceable channel of negotiation—has become even more serious in these days. Nuclear arms are now more numerous and more destructive, and the vehicles that carry them are multiple and more accurate.

The arms buildup has become more uncontrolled and, as if this weren't enough, attempts are being made to extend the field of military confrontation to space.

The number of regional hot spots has increased and imperialist intervention in them is now greater and more direct than ever before.

Unequal international economic relations, which gave rise in Belgrade to the action program drawn up by the underdeveloped countries meeting there, are far from reduced. Instead, they have

This speech by Fidel Castro to the Eighth Summit Conference of the Movement of Nonaligned Countries was given on behalf of the Latin American Group during the official ceremony marking the 25th anniversary of the founding of the Movement.

'The African National Congress and its dedicated fighters deserve the glory for having inspired the unflinching struggle of the South African people and having shown that now as yesterday and tomorrow and always, nothing can stop the march of history and no force on earth can shackle human dignity and freedom indefinitely.'

become even more bitterly unbearable for our weak and backward economies. The foreign debt has become an intolerable burden that makes impossible the crystallization of all our efforts and sacrifices toward development. The purchasing power of our products and raw materials is lower now than it was then. Our peoples are overwhelmed by poverty. Disease and ignorance, monstrous by-products of economic backwardness, are rampant in Asia, Africa and Latin America.

Problems and dangers have increased, and with them our power to resist, our strength and our struggle. This also gives our celebration greater force.

In 1961 our Movement consisted of 25 countries. On the eve of the Eighth Summit Conference we have grown to 101. Many of those who are here with us today and who are still determined to resist and struggle were fighting for their independence 25 years ago. Robert Mugabe, who is presiding over our meeting with all his experience and serenity, and other distinguished heads of state here with us today were then attending our summit conference as representatives of an aspiration to independence that is now an encouraging reality.

We haven't just grown in terms of number, having now become the absolute majority of the UN and the international community, but also history has demonstrated the validity of our program, the just nature of our aspirations and the need to reach our goals so that the world can move toward a safer and happier future.

We came into being in 1961 as a result of the national liberation process of struggle against colonialism in many countries. The indestructible link between that historic battle against colonialism and the peaceful aspirations of the peoples was set down as the first postulate of the Belgrade Conference. The postulate states that in order for there to be lasting peace, as a result of the confrontation between the old structures and the new, emerging nationalist forces, the development, as was then explained, of "a world in which the domination of colonialism and imperialism in all their manifestations is radically eliminated," was indispensable.

The First Summit also clearly stipulated that "basically the elimination of sources of conflict means the elimination of colonialism."

Likewise, when it came into being, our Movement advocated "the immediate unconditional, total and definitive elimination of colonialism, and the concerted effort to end all forms of neocolonialism and imperialist domination in all their forms and manifestations."

When Paragraph No. 21 of the Belgrade Declaration called for "the elimination of economic inequality inherited from colonialism and imperialism," it was laying the groundwork for a program which the Movement would set forth years later when it stressed the need for a new international economic order and endorsed the charter of rights and duties of states.

Nothing demonstrates better the penetrating foresight of Tito, Nehru, Nasser, Nkrumah and other founders of the Movement than the present-day confirmation and implementation of those aims (now more elaborated and updated), reflected in the draft declaration of Harare which we will discuss.

There can be no better tribute to their memory as we gather here in Harare—then under colonial rule and now a symbol of Africa still threatened by imperialism and its most despicable tool, racist and fascist South Africa—than the power, prestige and current influence of this mighty grouping of states, with different systems and viewpoints but united behind the fundamental principles of the Movement: peace, independence, development and the struggle against imperialism, colonialism, neocolonialism, and racism and its most sinister form: apartheid.

The fact that 25 years after the Movement was founded and in spite of our victories over over colonialism we are still only beginning to make real that just program of mobilization, demonstrates what the Movement was able to confirm a few years later at the Second Summit in Cairo when it noted that "the forces of imperialism are still powerful and do not hesitate to resort to violence to defend their interests and uphold their privileges."

Twenty-five years later we are threatened by the arms race and space war. Namibia is still occupied by the South African racists who also attack all the Front Line States. The Palestinians lack the state to which they have a right. Nicaragua must face up to the aggression which the United States government obstinately refuses to halt, in spite of the Contadora and Support Groups' efforts.

In Harare most of the Belgrade program still remains ahead of us, but our quarter century of struggle has had visible results.

As the unforgettable President Tito noted with insight in 1964, "With its progressive action in the common struggle with the socialist countries and other forces, the Movement has become one of the important factors in the current balance of forces."

If we unite, no decision can be made at the United Nations or in the international community as a whole that does not take us into account. Combining our forces with all those who in Europe, Japan and North America itself oppose any decision leading to war will allow us to stop those who want to unleash it. The military pacts that divide the most powerful nations into hostile blocs are, as is acknowledged, an anachronism which must be eliminated.

That is why we have convened here at the Eighth Summit.

On speaking here as an honorable assignment given me by the representatives of the sister nations of Latin America and the Caribbean, I can say our peoples concur in the endorsement of these noble goals. The unity of our lands called for by Simón Bolívar at the dawn of independence and again dreamed of at the end of the century by José Martí, now has added reasons to come about.

The Malvinas War reminded Latin Americans that the freedom of their peoples cannot depend on a powerful neighbor who stalks them and it must necessarily be based on their combative efforts. Cuba was the only Latin American country that signed the Belgrade Act: Bolivia, Brazil and Ecuador were present as observers. Now there are 17 Latin American and Caribbean countries in the Movement and nine more as observers. Thus we can safely say the nonaligned enjoy growing support and understanding in the countries of our region.

We confirm that support and do so with the certainty that nuclear disaster will be avoided. That ways will be found to achieve the definitive end of nuclear testing—which one of the sides is already willing to undertake—thereby leading to substantive and far-reaching negotiations to end the arms race and reduce conventional weapons to a minimum so that man can eliminate nuclear weapons from the face of the earth rather than one day having nuclear weapons eliminate him from the face of the earth. We are also certain that the backwardness and poverty caused by the economic inequality that plagues us can be overcome through joint action.

This is the goal to which we are inspired by the memory of that unforgettable event 25 years ago.

We will do honor to that date by being true to the principles that have brought us to this historic meeting in Harare.

Thank you very much.

'The Third World debt is unpayable and
uncollectable; it is politically, economically and
morally impossible for these countries to pay; our
countries are not debtors, but creditors; the
development of capitalism was financed with the
blood, sweat and wealth of the colonies in Asia,
Africa and Latin America.'

The Third World debt is unpayable and uncollectable

Esteemed Chairman Robert Mugabe; Distinguished heads of state and government; Delegates; Distinguished guests;

Only seven years ago, at the Sixth Summit Conference held in Havana, we had the honor to welcome the heroic liberation movement of Zimbabwe, a country that had yet to win its independence, as a new member of the Movement of Nonaligned Countries. Today, the Eighth Summit Conference in Harare, Africa's youngest sovereign state and front line in the struggle against racism and apartheid, symbolizes the strength of our Movement and the peoples' inexorable march toward independence.

In electing Zimbabwe to host the Eighth Summit Conference, we also elected the man who was to chair the Movement for this new term, the national hero who led his people to their struggle for liberation: Robert Mugabe.

Esteemed Comrade Mugabe, allow me, on behalf of Cuba, to add my respect and affection to that with which this meeting welcomes you. We are certain that, under your experienced, serious leadership, the Movement of Nonaligned Countries will make far-reaching decisions at this meeting and take firm steps for the future.

On this occasion, I also wish to pay tribute to the memory of one

This speech by Fidel Castro to the Eighth Summit Conference of the Movement of Nonaligned Countries held in Harare, Zimbabwe was presented on September 2, 1986.

who leaves a great absence: the unforgettable Indira Gandhi. She led us wisely and with dignity for most of the presidential mandate entrusted to India. We were all deeply shaken by her heinous assassination. We will always remember her with profound respect and gratitude. In paying tribute to her, I also draw attention to what Prime Minister Rajiv Gandhi's calm, wise leadership has meant to the nonaligned. He upheld the Movement's independence and kept us united in difficult times. Under his wise leadership, we progressed steadily toward this summit meeting.

Our world faces two hitherto unknown, deadly dilemmas: peace or complete self-destruction; a just international economic order or the most horrifying future for the immense majority of the peoples represented here, even were there to be peace.

Our peoples of the Third World are the ones who are threatened by the worst of both dilemmas: we can be wiped off the face of the earth in a war for which we are not responsible and in which we will not take part, and we can be crushed by hunger and poverty because of a world economic order that we did not create and that came into being and developed in spite of and against our will.

Many years ago, speaking at the UN, I said, "Let the philosophy of plunder cease and the philosophy of war will cease."

That philosophy of plunder, pillage and exploitation of other peoples was the basis for the conquest and colonization of last century, at the cost of the peoples of America, Africa and Asia. A handful of European powers raped, killed, massacred and uprooted tens of millions of people from their lands to enslave them. From our soil, those powers took all the gold and silver they could get their hands on; and from the sweat and toil of their slaves, they obtained tons of sugar, coffee, cacao, tea, cotton and other products to be enjoyed by their colonial societies. This is how capitalism was born, oozing blood from all its pores, and this is how imperialism and necolonialism followed later.

There's no need to study this in any Marxist book, because it's written in indelible marks on the flesh of all our peoples.

What is underdevelopment if not the end product of that historical plunder?

The two World Wars, that signified such rivers of blood for humanity, arose from the philosophy of plunder, the old repartition and attempted new repartitions of the world among the imperialist powers. That same philosophy is behind imperialism today unleashing the greatest arms buildup ever in the annals of history.

The developed capitalist powers cannot resign themselves to

losing our natural resources, raw materials, markets and cheap labor. They cannot accept the fact they can no longer sell their products at ever higher prices, while paying increasingly lower prices for ours. They refuse to give up the systematic plunder of our economies. They cannot resign themselves to the existence of forms of production and distribution of social wealth other than those of their obsolete and rotten capitalism. In short, they cannot resign themselves to the existence of real national independence in their former colonies and a people's liberation movement.

This is the main reason for the enormous accumulation of nuclear arsenals, strategic missiles, long-range bombers, giant aircraft carriers, battleships, submarines, rapid deployment forces and imperialist military bases the world over. This is the reason for the frenzied efforts to deploy weapons in space, so that one day man will not even be able to look at the stars without the view being shrouded by the thought that he's surrounded by a deadly arsenal of nuclear arms, laser rays, particle beams and similar devices. No country in the world will be able to feel safe. Space weapons have no other objective than robbing man of his possessions on earth. This is why the imperialists refuse to abide by the law of the sea, drawn up and approved by the immense majority of the international community. They want for themselves all the oceans and all the minerals in the seabed within reach of their sophisticated technology.

No one should be surprised by my calling things by their name. Should the United States achieve the world military predominance it so desperately seeks, all those present here know that their oil, iron, copper, chromium, bauxite, rubber, lead, zinc and other natural resources and raw materials would again be divided up among the big capitalist powers, to satisfy their insatiable consumer hunger, and we wouldn't have a single weapon with which to defend ourselves.

This didn't happen at the time of the oil crisis, simply because of the existence of a new balance of forces since the birth of socialism and the over 100 countries that have freed themselves from the yoke of colonialism.

Cuba, a founding member of the Nonaligned Movement, is proud to be a socialist country.

The very essence of socialism is alien to war and to exploiting the sweat and toil of peoples and their natural resources. Socialism has no need to invest abroad, to have military bases beyond its borders or divide up the world. It does not need to produce weapons in order to boost the economy and make monopolies rich. It knows perfectly well that resources can and should be invested in factories, hospitals, schools, housing, recreational and cultural centers and other worthy projects. Arms spending is the heaviest burden imposed on socialism by imperialism. Our country, only a few miles from the United States, is fully aware of this.

At this hour of decisive importance for all peoples, it is precisely imperialism and not socialism that refuses to put an end to nuclear tests and rejects the only coherent, logical and acceptable policy for all humanity: that is, the cessation of the arms buildup, the banning of chemical warfare and other means of mass destruction, a significant reduction in conventional weapons and the implementation of a program for the total eradication of nuclear arms in the shortest possible time.

This aspiration is shared not only by the people who are building socialism but by every responsible and sane person on earth.

The nightmare that weighs on humankind must come to an end.

No one can speak of security in a world that could be exterminated at any moment of the day or night. And if humanity is to have a bearing on events that determine its very existence, including the people in the imperialist countries, it must make these objectives prevail through the international community.

Peace is one of our Movement's most sacred duties. No one is exempt from this obligation. In the meeting held recently in Mexico, the group composed of six eminent international figures said that peace was a task not only for the big powers but also for all the world's peoples.

Humanity can and should be able to impose peace. The Movement of Nonaligned Countries, given its immense prestige and political strength, can and should make a decisive contribution in this direction.

The other deadly dilemma pressing upon us, that is, the economic dilemma, is yet another threat to our survival. However, in this case, the countries of the Third World are practically its only victims.

This is why we need not only peace but also that the resources destined to war and to the destruction of man be diverted to the world's economic and social development, first of all the historically plundered countries, the former colonies, the new colonies of today. However, whereas at the time of the Summit Conference in New Delhi, in 1983, military expenditure ran to over $650 billion, in 1985 the figure was $850 billion, despite the fact that today the nuclear arsenal is equal to almost 16 billion tons of TNT: in other words, enough to exterminate the world's population 12 times over.

Since World War II, that is, in the space of only 40 years, military expenditure has amounted to $17 trillion. The figure is much higher than that which would have been needed for developing all the Third World countries. Today, we wouldn't have the billions of hungry, undernourished, illiterate, sick, unemployed people we have in the world. Today, our countries' astronomical foreign debt of almost a trillion dollars—which, while overwhelming, represents only 5.8 percent of postwar arms spending—would not exist.

As I said at the UN after the Sixth Summit Meeting. "The rattle of weapons, threatening language and arrogance on the international scene must cease. Enough of the illusion that the world's problems can be solved by means of nuclear weapons. Bombs may kill the hungry, the sick and the ignorant, but they cannot kill hunger, disease and ignorance. Nor can they kill the righteous rebellion of the peoples—and in the holocaust, the rich, who are the ones who have the most to lose in this world, will also die."

There can be no development without peace nor can there be peace without development for the immense majority of the world's peoples.

The fact is that we're being exploited in an increasingly merciless fashion. We have to pay increasingly higher prices for what we import from the developed capitalist world—it could be a truck, a tractor, a locomotive, an industrial component, a factory, a medicine, some type of equipment or a simple spare part—but we're getting increasingly lower prices for what we export.

With the exception of oil—the privilege of a handful of countries which are also having troubles—we must now export three, four and even six times more sugar, tea, coffee, cacao, agave, copra, iron, bauxite, copper etc., in exchange for the same product imported 30 years ago.

Today there's more unequal trade, more protectionism, more dumping, more unfair competition, more market control by the transnationals, higher interest rates, more flight of capital to the U.S. and European financial centers, and more manipulation of international finance by the imperialist powers than ever before. The price we're paying as neocolonies is much higher than the one we paid even when we were colonies.

It is not my intention to overwhelm you with figures, but allow

121

me to quote a few to illustrate this tragic situation.

The foreign debt ran to $373 billion in 1977. In 1985, only eight years later, it was three times as much, that is, $950 billion.

Between 1981 and 1985, the Third World countries laid out over $300 billion in interest alone and $526 billion for the full servicing of the debt.

In 1985, Africa spent 32 percent of its export earnings on servicing the debt, and Latin America, 44 percent.

Between 1980 and 1985, the Third World countries lost $104 billion as a result of unfavorable terms of trade and $120 billion because of excessive interest rates. In 1985, the drop in the price of basic products forced those countries to deliver 25 percent more than they had delivered in 1980, in order to obtain the same amount of imports.

Whereas in 1979, 40.2 percent of the international flow of finance went to the Third World countries, in 1985 those countries received only 10.3 percent. In 1980, the United States—the world's richest and most developed country—received 6.1 percent, but by 1985 the figure had risen to 24.2 percent. The losses due to the flight of capital as a result of chronic inflation, the high interest rates levied by the U.S. banks, and insecurity in the countries of origin are incalculable. The money needed for the United States' colossal rearmament, star wars, gigantic budget and trade deficits, policy of aggression and other insane aspects of the United States' present administration had to come from somewhere.

The International Monetary Fund—imperialism's financial gendarme—demands that the Third World countries put an end to budget and trade deficits, make cuts in education and health, discontinue state investments, depreciate their currency, raise the price of consumer articles and services, and suspend restrictions on free imports. In other words, the burden of the debt and the crisis is to be shouldered by the already impoverished people. However, in Washington, only a few blocks from the IMF head offices, stands the White House, the home of the U.S. government which has incurred the most fabulous and most incredible fiscal and trade deficits known to world history. Despite its proximity, the IMF has never sent an expert to the White House to demand an end to fiscal deficits, unequal trade, protectionism, dumping, high interest rates, the manipulation of the dollar and other infamous practices with such disastrous effects on the world economy.

Nor does it send experts to the countries of the European

Economic Community, which flood the world with subsidized agricultural products in disloyal competition with Third World countries, displaying a selfishness verging on madness.

The United States rearms with the world's money, and the Monetary Fund keeps silent. The United States lives and spends beyond its production levels at the expense of the world economy, and the Monetary Fund keeps silent. Such is the economic order that has been imposed on us.

With the help of mathematics, we have analyzed all possible variations suggested to help solve the debt problem: with current or lower interest rates, with or without new loans, with payment limits tied to exports or without such limits, and even considering the virtually utopian case of rapid, sustained development. The results of all the analyses are that the debt, like a huge and monstrous cancer whose malignant cells multiply quickly, tends to reproduce itself and grow indefinitely.

One day it occurred to us to calculate how much time it would take a single man to count the Latin American foreign debt at the rate of a dollar a second, and it proved to be more than 12,000 years. At present there is a disease which is much talked about and very worrisome: Acquired Immune Deficiency Syndrome. Well, the Third World foreign debt is the AIDS of the world economy.

From the mathematical analyses and serious reflection on the problem, we concluded that the Third World foreign debt is unpayable and uncollectable; that it is politically, economically and morally impossible for these countries to pay; that our countries are not debtors, but creditors; that the development of capitalism was financed with the blood, sweat and wealth of the colonies in Asia, Africa and Latin America; that through unequal terms of trade they have stolen from us much more than what the total of the debt amounts to; that protectionism and dumping block our exports and ruin our peoples; that much of the money lent us returned to the Western financial centers without benefiting our peoples in any way; that the excessively high interest rates multiply the already unbearable burden; that the foreign debt must be cancelled; that the governments of creditor countries must assume the debt with their own banks, without any need for new taxes or sacrifices of any kind for depositors or taxpayers in those countries; that with less than 15 percent of current yearly military spending the debt could soon be paid; and that the world economy can only overcome the crisis with the abolition of the debt and the institution of the new international economic order, which has been approved by the UN and never implemented. This would mean an increase of hundreds of billions a year in the purchasing power of the Third World, thereby multiplying international trade. Moreover, it would set the industries of the developed capitalist countries running at full capacity and help them mitigate their worst tragedy: chronic and growing unemployment.

To prove that the resources exist, it is enough to point out that in 1988 the developed capitalist countries will save at least $120 billion as a result of lower oil prices. That would be enough to cover Third World debt servicing for this year. With less than a third of the sum wasted on military spending a year, it would be possible to abolish the debt and also cover the cost of the new international economic order.

Peace, disarmament, a solution to the foreign debt and the new international economic order are thus inseparable issues. If the statesmen of the developed capitalist countries fail to see it that way, they will be recognizing that their economic and social system is obsolete, selfish, irrational and totally incapable of helping to solve the problems of today's world.

We can't sit by with arms crossed. We must demand solutions because we have a right to survive the dangers that threaten us and to live in dignity and peace. José Martí, Cuba's National Hero, said something once that could serve as the motto for this meeting: "Rights are taken, not asked for; they are wrested, not begged for."

We represent the great majority of humanity and should not beg for our right to life; we must be capable of wresting it.

Distinguished heads of state or government, the young states and national liberation movements attend these summits in the hope that their just causes will be defended. Seldom has one of our meetings aroused such hopes.

Representatives of the FMLN of El Salvador, of the National Revolutionary Union of Guatemala and of the brave and militant people of President Allende have come here from our continent. In El Salvador, more than 50,000 deaths as a result of ferocious repression; in Guatemala, a country where there have never been political prisoners, 80,000 people have disappeared since the CIA overthrew Arbenz in 1954 and imposed various military regimes. In Chile, thousands of people were killed or have disappeared and the people are brutally repressed and yet are determined to overcome fascism; in Grenada, a country invaded to crush a revolution that had already destroyed itself; in Puerto Rico, a portion of Latin America under colonial rule and occupation; in Paraguay, a fascist dictatorship that has already lasted more than 30 years; these are some examples of the fruits of U.S. intervention on our balkanized continent.

Wherever a genocidal and corrupt government sprang up in Latin America, there was the United States backing it. Wherever there was social change, wherever the peoples wanted to be truly free, they have always come up against the hostility, blockades and acts of aggression of the United States. Cuba, part of whose soil is still occupied by the United States and has been subjected to more than 25 years of brutal economic blockade, is an exceptional witness to this reality.

However, Nicaragua is the most recent and eloquent example of the empire's brutal policy: nearly 50 years of the Somozas tyranny as a result of U.S. military intervention and the total support of the United States in the closest alliance. The new Nicaragua, which came into being as a result of the heroism of its sons and daughters, is the victim of a dirty, outrageous war of aggression: its economy is blockaded and its ports are mined; thousands of mercenaries at the service of a foreign power invade its soil from Honduras, which the government of the United States has turned into a sanctuary for the counterrevolution, a foreign military base and a springboard for attack against a sister nation.

The United States' dirty war has already resulted in the loss of tens of thousands of lives and billions of dollars in Nicaragua. Latin America's efforts to achieve peace in Central America through the Contadora Group have been shattered by U.S. determination to drown the Sandinista revolution in a bloodbath and crush the liberation movement in Central America. In an open and shameless manner, like a slap in the face for the peoples of Latin America and the world, the government of the United States recently secured approval of another $100 million to continue its bloody adventure against Nicaragua, thereby trampling on the verdict of the International Court at The Hague, which categorically condemned such actions. However, nothing will work. No force will be able to crush the resolute spirit and heroism of the Nicaraguan people even if the tragic lesson of Vietnam has to be repeated there.

Nicaragua has offered its hospitable and heroic soil as the venue for the Ninth Summit. Supporting it would be a gesture of solidarity. Today Nicaragua is not only a symbol of the struggle for independence in a Central American country but also of the independence struggle of the peoples of an entire continent, a symbol of the right of any Third World country to be the master of its destiny.

The British occupation of the Malvinas, which is part of the Argentine Republic, is an affront to the peoples of America. Latin American blood was shed there in the struggle against a NATO power, which enjoyed the support of the United States, as was to be expected.

Nobody should be confused about the Malvinas. There is no nation there such as Guyana or Belize; there is no community there that seeks autonomy or independence. They are inhabited by a handful of British settlers who consider themselves British and want to remain British. It is a colonial enclave, a foreign possession, an occupied territory that should be returned to Argentina.

The people of Peru have been victimized by the arbitrary measures taken by the International Monetary Fund and also require our resolute support.

Panama expects our permanent support so that the Canal agreements are respected.

Bolivia demands and deserves support for its just aspiration to an outlet to the sea through land that belonged to it.

In their desire for freedom and for their just causes, the peoples of Latin America expect the wholehearted support and solidarity of the Movement of Nonaligned Countries.

In the Middle East and northern Africa, Cuba has been, is and will always be in solidarity with the just struggle of the Arab peoples, who are the victims of imperialist and Zionist aggression. It firmly supports the PLO and endorses the noble cause of the Palestinian people and their right to independence, their country and a nation state; these rights can't be ignored forever, nor will peace in the Middle East be possible as long as these monstrous injustices continue.

We must support the sovereignty, unity and peace of the brave Lebanese people; the integrity of Cyprus; the dedicated and admirable struggle of the Saharawi people for their unquestionable and inalienable right to national independence. It is difficult to explain why the Saharawi Arab Democratic Republic has not been incorporated into our Movement. Its people also face the most modern weapons which U.S. imperialism gives the foreign occupants.

The Libyan Arab nation was recently the victim of a bloody provocation by the United States and a criminal, treacherous Nazi-style attack against its people. We have witnessed how the government of the United States is capable of using its most sophisticated weapons to try to murder a head of state and his family. Our Movement must strongly condemn such infamous terrorist practices.

The war between Iran and Iraq, two member states of our Movement, should never have broken out. Unfortunately, all efforts to find a solution to this difficult and complex conflict have proved fruitless, but we must not flag in our efforts to achieve peace and heal as much as possible the damage and wounds caused by the fratricidal conflict.

We firmly support efforts to find a negotiated political solution to the problem of Afghanistan, based on the strictest respect for the sovereignty of that country.

Likewise, we forcefully support the just and sacred struggle of the Democratic People's Republic of Korea for peaceful reunification of its country, artificially divided and partially occupied by the United States.

We have made it very clear that the next Olympic Games should be shared between North and South. If this doesn't happen, our country will not participate in an event irresponsibly prepared to legitimize one of the most repressive and discredited regimes in the world, while the Democratic People's Republic of Korea was completely ignored. There must be express solidarity with this sister nation's legitimate aspiration in this regard.

We also join in the just demand for an Indian Ocean free of foreign naval bases and nuclear weapons.

I have left southern Africa for last.

We are here, not very many miles from the sinister apartheid system. On the other side of Zimbabwe's southern border, more than 25 million people, who constitute the great majority of the country's population, are deprived of the most elementary human rights. Every day the news coming from there tells of terrible murders committed against the people.

More than four decades after the defeat of fascism and its racist theories, which took the lives of over 40 million people and on the eve of the 21st century, a state segregates its citizens and is built on racial foundations.

To this racism we must add the most ferocious economic exploitation of the oppressed, segregated and discriminated-against masses.

Apartheid is the direct consequence of the colonial system and the brutal way in which the African peoples were forcibly deprived of their lands and natural resources and their sons and daughters enslaved and sold all over the world. Apartheid has kept itself going only thanks to the backing of the United States and other NATO countries which view South Africa as a strategic ally, a source of raw materials, a market for investment and of lucrative profits for the transnationals at the cost of the sweat and blood of millions of Africans.

The current administration in the United States categorically refuses to accept economic sanctions against South Africa and systematically vetoes the Security Council resolution that would affect the Pretoria regime. Meanwhile, it imposes stricter and stricter economic blockades on small progressive or revolutionary countries such as Cuba, Nicaragua, Vietnam, Libya and the Democratic People's Republic of Korea.

Encouraged by the support it gets from the so-called constructive engagement of the U.S. government, South Africa not only defies the world by continuing to harden apartheid but also maintains the illegal occupation of Namibia and prevents the independence of that country under colonial rule, in open defiance of all UN resolutions and agreements.

South Africa organizes mercenary bands to destabilize neighboring states and carries out treacherous surprise attacks against Lesotho, Botswana, Zimbabwe, Zambia and Angola. It violates the N'komati agreement with Mozambique by continuing its support for subversive groups. Now the United States has joined in these destabilization plans and has brought to Africa the sinister methods used in Latin America, with open, shameless support for the UNITA bands in Angola.

UNITA has a long history of cooperation with the colonialists and imperialists. It was created by the Portuguese political police during the Angolan liberation war to sabotage the patriotic effort. With its help, South Africa tried to destroy Angola's independence in 1975 and dismember the country. It has used UNITA as its tool during the last ten years in its dirty war against Angola.

When we were children, we were told in school that two things equal to a third one were themselves the same. By upholding the same banners as the UNITA bands and giving them joint support the governments of the United States and South Africa express their affinity of ideas and aims and are themselves the same.

What difference can there be between the policies of Washington and Pretoria? As far as the U.S. government is concerned, the Palestinians evicted from the land where they lived for thousands of years, the admirable Saharawi fighters, the brave fighters of the ANC, the patriots of SWAPO and the heroic revolutionaries of El Salvador and Chile are terrorists who only deserve to be exterminated.

By contrast the UNITA bandits who destroy entire villages of defenseless civilians, be they women, men or children; the Somocista mercenary bands at the service of a foreign power; and any thugs who oppose a popular and progressive process are, in the eyes of that imperialist government, distinguished patriots and freedom fighters deserving of aid from the United States. Is this fascism or is it not? Is this racism or is it not? Is this cynicism or is it not?

Our solidarity with the African liberation movement and its heroic battles against colonialism, apartheid and racism isn't merely verbal.

In the struggles against Portuguese colonialism, Cuban revolutionaries fought alongside Amilcar Cabral and Agostinho Neto in Guinea-Bissau and Angola; some gave their lives in this noble cause. In 1975, when South Africa invaded Angola and occupied more than half of its territory, in spite of the fact that an entire ocean separates Cuba from Africa, Cuban internationalist fighters, along with their heroic Angolan brothers, battled the racist troops and forced them to retreat over 800 kilometers, to the border with Namibia, showing the world that South African soldiers, like those of Hitler, were by no means invincible.

In spite of the tremendous effort it entails for our small country, a contingent of tens of thousands of Cuban internationalist fighters has stood guard alongside the glorious Angolan armed forces for ten years so as to avoid a repetition of the events of 1975.

Our cooperation with Africa is not only military. More than 15,000 young Africans study in our country free of charge and thousands of Cuban doctors, teachers technicians and workers are serving on the continent free of charge. Over 250,000 of our fellow citizens have served in Africa on a military or civilian basis.

This absolutely unselfish gesture of solidarity disturbs the U.S. imperialists and South African racists. For them such cooperation among formerly conquered, colonized and enslaved nations that can build a mighty barrier to aggression is inconceivable.

Both the U.S. imperialists and the South African racists do all they can to secure the withdrawal of the Cuban internationalist forces from Angola, trying to link Namibian independence to this. By mutual agreement the governments of Angola and Cuba have responded by saying: implement UN Resolution No. 435 on Namibia;

halt the threat of aggression against Angola; end the dirty war and support for the mercenary bands, and a gradual and progressive withdrawal of 20,000 Cuban soldiers who defend strategic positions in southern Angola will start. The rest of the Cuban military personnel will only be withdrawn when the sovereign governments of Cuba and Angola see fit, with no conditions set.

The real crux of the matter is that as long as apartheid exists in South Africa, as long as that country is ruled by a racist and fascist government, there won't be any security for Angola or any other nation of southern Africa, and the independence of Namibia will be mere myth.

That's why I can categorically state here that the presence of Cuban troops in Angola is based on principles and not due to any type of Cuban national interest or questions of prestige. When apartheid is no more and when the fascist and racist regime has disappeared in South Africa, no country will feel threatened. Namibia will become free immediately and no Cuban soldiers will be needed. Then it will be possible to proceed immediately with a total withdrawal of Cuban forces from Angola. Of course, Angola, whose sovereignty we have always respected and will always respect with absolute loyalty, can decide at any time whether it does or does not need our military personnel there. What I have just expressed is our willingness to keep our troops in Angola as long as there is apartheid in South Africa.

I am sure that as an essential part of its contribution to the struggle for peace, development, justice and security in our world, our summit will give full support and its tremendous political and moral backing to the oppressed peoples of South Africa and Namibia and will go down in history for its decisive contribution to the final battle against apartheid. This monstrous regime cannot be reformed — it must be eliminated. It is now in the throes of an insurmountable crisis. The ANC and its dedicated fighters, heroic men and women like Nelson and Winnie Mandela, deserve the glory for having inspired the unflinching struggle of the South African people and having shown that now as yesterday and tomorrow and always, nothing can stop the march of history and no force on earth can shackle human dignity and freedom indefinitely.

Thank you.